24 QUILTED GEMS

Sparkling Traditional & Original Projects

GAI PERRY

C&T PUBLISHING

Dear Helen —
I Hope you
enjoy making
my favorite
Renet patterns —
Gai Perry
2003

© 2003 Gai Perry
Editor-in-Chief: Darra Williamson
Editor: Liz Aneloski
Technical Editors: Carolyn Aune, Joyce Lytle, Gailen Runge
Copyeditor: Linda D. Smith
Proofreader: Susan Nelsen
Design Director: Diane Pedersen
Book Design: Dawn DeVries Sokol
Cover Designer: Kristen Yenche
Illustrator: Richard Sheppard
Production Assistant: Tim Manibusan
Quilt Photography: Sharon Risedorph
Published by C&T Publishing, Inc., P.O. Box 1456, Lafayette, California 94549

Library of Congress Cataloging-in-Publication Data

Perry, Gai
  24 quilted gems : sparkling traditional & original projects / Gai Perry.
    p. cm.
  ISBN 1-57120-211-0 (paper trade)
  1. Patchwork--Patterns. 2. Quilting--Patterns. I. Title: Twenty four quilted gems. II. Title.
  TT835.P35225 2003
  746.46'041--dc21

                                   2003004310

Printed in China
10 9 8 7 6 5 4 3 2 1

A Note of Appreciation

I took an aptitude test in high school and was told never to get a job that involved working with numbers. So what did I do? I wrote a book that's filled with them.

Needless to say, I wouldn't have attempted it without constant hand-holding and technical assistance from Liz Aneloski, Carolyn Aune, and Joyce Lytle; the thoughtful, witty, intelligent, kind, and attractive editors and designers at C&T Publishing. THANK YOU!

Dedication

This book is dedicated to my two young granddaughters, Carly and Brenna. When they were staying with me, they often had the good grace to allow me to work at the computer, uninterrupted.

CONTENTS

INTRODUCTION

L et's face it. Quiltmaking is an addiction! It must be because how else can I explain the hundreds of hours I spend in quilt shops . . . and a fabric stash that could last through the next millennium? Don't laugh. If you've bought this book, you're probably a quilt-a-holic, too.

Well, now I've taken this compulsion one step further. Not only am I addicted to making quilts, I've become addicted to writing about them. As each of my books is published, I heave a sigh of relief and tell myself that enough is enough. It's time to smell the roses, take a vacation, paint some pictures, paint the house, paint my nails. But do I listen to what I'm saying? No! The printer's ink was barely dry on *Do-It-Yourself Framed Quilts* before I started thinking about what to write next. And this time it didn't take long to come up with an idea. All I had to do was look at the stacks of quilt pattern requests I've received over the years.

I've never written satisfactory replies to these letters because I don't work with a rotary cutter or employ quick-cutting and sewing techniques. I'm a template and scissors gal through and through. Because of these old-fashioned methods, it would take hours to develop a pattern that a modern quilter like yourself could live with—and I wasn't willing to spare the time. My inadequate response to these requests has always been to write a note saying that I didn't have a pattern, but someday I would include it in a book.

And now I'm happy to say that *someday* has arrived! This book contains my most-requested quilt patterns along with up-to-date cutting methods and more how-to information than you could possibly want or need. I've also included design and size variations of each quilt so you can pick the one that's right for you.

Many of these by-request quilt patterns are my favorites too, and as you interpret them with your own special blend of vision and style, I hope you will come to love them as much as I do!

AN ARTISTIC APPROACH

When I started quilting, I joined a guild and began attending monthly lectures. One of the first speakers I heard was a quilter whose entire motivation was to make a quilt as quickly as possible. She was enthralled with her ability to turn out a bed-size quilt top in a day. She gave us a trunk show of her speedy creations and shared some quick-piecing tips. Even as a novice I could see that her quilts were less than spectacular and I was annoyed that I had to spend an hour of my time listening to her.

Later that night, as I lay in bed, I was still grumbling to myself. I didn't think quilting was an experience that needed to be hurried. But then a light bulb went off in my head! I realized that lightning-speed quiltmaking was her particular joy and her primary reason for quilting. Once I understood that, I was able to appreciate the pleasure she derived. The fact that her quilts contained very few colors and fabrics was unimportant. All that mattered was beating the clock. She was a happy quilter! What I'm trying to say is that each of us has a quiltmaking agenda. When I understood her point of view, it made me want to define my own approach to quilting.

To me, quilting is an art, not a craft that can be reduced to mathematical formulas. I like to design on a vertical surface, much like an artist working at an easel. Usually, I create the whole quilt top on my design wall before I take the first stitch. It's the pleasure of watching it grow, like a painting in progress, that keeps me interested.

With my quiltmaking priorities identified, I was able to eliminate all the stuff that was driving me crazy. Strip piecing and quick cutting hundreds of triangles that often went unused were the first things to go. I made a master set of templates and cut fabric only as needed. It was totally liberating! I began concentrating on simple quilt patterns with complex color and fabric harmonies. What bliss! It seems that *my* joy of quilting depends on how much visual stimulation I can get into a quilt—not how fast I can make it.

Now I'm not suggesting that my approach is right for you. Once you analyze your own quilting priorities you'll probably find that your comfort level lies somewhere between the speedy quilter I mentioned earlier and my slower, more *painterly* method. But for the sake of comparison, why not experience the design phase of quiltmaking from an artist's point of view? Once you see a quilt top develop as an entire entity rather than a series of unrelated units, your design skills will blossom—and certainly, you will begin to feel more comfortable with your color and fabric selections.

FABRIC, COLOR, DESIGN & EQUIPMENT

FABRIC

Fabric can be soft . . . crisp . . . nubby . . . smooth . . . warm . . . or cool. It can be bright . . . dull . . . dark . . . or light. It is infused with rainbows—and each piece can tell you its history by the motif that is printed on its surface. Fabric is the very essence of quiltmaking!

There is almost nothing I like better than shopping for fabric. Just walking into a quilt shop can make me shiver with anticipation. I prefer 100% cottons, but occasionally I'll purchase a polyester blend because of its distinctive color or print style. Of course nowadays, anything goes. Quilters are enthusiastically combining wools, silks, and synthetics and I admire their sense of adventure.

Fabric Scraps

Most of these by-request patterns can be identified as *scrap quilts*. Scrap or (make-do) quilts were originally made out of necessity due to the scarcity of yard goods in early America. Women pieced together fragments of worn-out clothing and odd bits of yardage and by some miracle, these unrelated scraps came together to create thousands of stunningly inventive quilts. Lucky us! Today, we have an endless source of fabric for our scrap quilts.

Almost any quilt block or overall pattern can be interpreted with scraps and one of the keys to making a scrappy-looking quilt is that no fabric or color should be repeated in the same place in each block. Challenging? Yes, but look at it as an opportunity to stretch your design choices and explore your fabric stash. And you know the old saying about how "less is more?" It definitely *doesn't* apply to scrap quilts!

Fabric Quantities

Suggested fabric amounts are given wherever possible, but because of the nature of scrap quilts, it's difficult to estimate accurate quantities. Actually, yardage amounts are unimportant because if and when you run out of a particular fabric, just use something else. That's all part of the serendipitous charm of scrap quilts.

When you are organizing fabrics for a quilt, pull from your stash, then if you need to buy fabric (for areas other than borders), purchase ⅛ or ¼ yards only.

Fabric Preparation

To prewash or not to prewash? That is the question. There are two schools of thought here and I lean toward the one that says don't bother. I like to wash a quilt after it's finished because I think the slight shrinkage gives added body and texture. When I make a wallhanging, I prefer *not* to wash it (ever if possible). The manufacturer's sizing helps to keep the colors from fading. I do, however, suggest testing any suspicious fabrics (such as solid reds) for colorfastness. Snip off a small piece and stick it in a glass of warm water. If the water changes color, the fabric must be treated with undiluted white vinegar or Retayne.

Cutting the Fabrics

Resist cutting all of a project's fabrics before you start designing. It is preferable to cut fabrics as needed. That way, the design possibilities are expanded and fabrics aren't wasted.

COLOR

A quilt with an attractive color scheme is like a friendly smile—it catches your attention and makes you want a closer look.

It would be naive to assume that the color suggestions for each quilt pattern will be used without changes. I'm sure that your personal color palette will influence your choices. But unless you were born with an artist's eye (or an intuitive knowledge of color theory), learning to feel secure with your choices takes patience and practice. Here are some suggestions that may help.

Start a Clip File

Look for magazine photos of quilts, landscapes, garden settings, room décor—anything that has an appealing combination of colors. I've been adding to my clip file for years and it's my main source of color inspiration.

Use a Focus Fabric

Find a printed fabric with several colors that appeal to you. Make a list of the colors and then select accompanying fabrics in those colors. The assortment should include a range of dark, medium, and light values and a variety of print styles. This is a foolproof method for developing a color scheme and even the most experienced quilters are not above using it.

Work With The Six Color Families

Most of you are familiar with the artists' Twelve-Color Circle, but learning how to make it work for you can be mysterious and sometimes, daunting. I prefer to simplify the circle by dividing it into six main groups: yellow, orange, red, purple, blue, and green. In each of these groups, or *Color Families*, there is a range of colors. The Red Color Family, for example, includes warm orange-reds through lustrous red-violets.

When it comes time to choose a color scheme, work with Color Families rather than individual shades of a color. The resulting quilt will look richer and more like the work of an accomplished quilt artist.

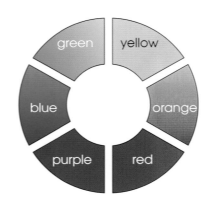

The Six Color Families

Learn To Recognize Value Contrast

Establishing light, medium, and dark areas is one of the most important elements in quilt design. But which color is lighter? Which is darker? These questions require constant re-examination because value is a *relative* term. A tint of lime green could be the lightest color in one quilt, and the darkest color in another quilt. Because the value of a color keeps changing, depending on what sits next to it, I have elected to use the words lighter and darker (instead of light and dark) in many of the project instructions. I've done this to remind you of the flexibility of value determination.

The easiest way to see the relative value of a group of colors is to stand back and squint your eyes. Doing this seems to accentuate the darks and lights. Also, try using a reducing glass. The merits of this delightful tool are discussed on page 11.

Rely On Harmonious Color Combinations

There are certain color combinations that have a built-in success rate. Why not try using some of your favorite colors in one of the following combinations?

Complementary: Color Families that appear *opposite* each other on the color circle—reds and greens, yellows and purples, blues and oranges.

Analogous: Color Families that appear *next* to each other on the color circle. Choose two or three Color Families—yellows, oranges, and reds; reds, purples, and blues; blues, greens, and yellows.

Monochromatic: Tints, tones, and shades from *one* Color Family.

Neutrals: Grays, tans, rosy beiges, and white. The different tints and tones of these neutral colors are infinite.

Here's my best advice. When you think about a color scheme for a quilt, it is important to consider colors that "speak to you!" How can you possibly like the finished quilt if the colors don't touch your heart?

DESIGN

The design or quilt pattern you select isn't nearly as important as the fabrics and colors you choose to interpret it.

I generally don't make an effort to create elaborate or complicated quilt designs. Most of my patterns are simple combinations of squares and triangles. This allows the colors and fabrics to be the main attraction. Sometimes a fabric or a combination of colors will inspire a design, but more often than not, I look at quilts from previous centuries. This is easy to do because there are so many books containing photographs of antique quilts.

Frequently, my designs are inspired by collections of museum-reproduction prints that are so popular now. I also enjoy interpreting traditional quilt patterns with contemporary fabrics. The framed Ocean Waves quilt on page 44 is a good example.

Design Wall

My method of quiltmaking requires a vertical design surface. If you have an eight-foot section of wall in your sewing room, you can create the ultimate design space with a minimum of disruption. Purchase five yards of Thermolam batting. (It comes in 45" widths.) Cut it in half across the width and, with a staple gun, attach the two halves to the empty wall area. (Line up the edges just as if you were putting up wallpaper.) Pieces of fabric will adhere to the Thermolam without the need for pinning. Later on, if you need to remove the batting from the wall, the tiny staple holes will hardly show.

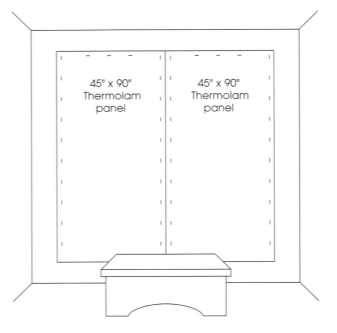

This is a sketch of my design wall. I climb on the antique blanket chest to reach the top.

Design Board

If you don't have the wall space, the next best thing is a portable design board. Purchase a 40" x 60" foamcore board from an art or office supply store. Get a yard of white cotton flannel to cover the board and attach it with straight pins. Even when you can't fit the whole quilt design on the board, at least you can critique the developing blocks.

Flannel-Covered Design Board

EQUIPMENT

Sharp scissors and a new blade in your rotary cutter . . . these two items will do more to enhance your quiltmaking skills than hundreds of dollars worth of fancy gadgets!

◆ I find it absolutely painful to watch a student trying to cut with dull scissors or sawing on a piece of fabric with her rotary cutter. Not only does it slow her down, it discourages her creativity. I buy the best quality scissors available and when they start to get dull, I don't even bother to get them sharpened—I buy a new pair. It's my one quiltmaking extravagance and it's worth every penny!

◆ For the same reason I've mentioned above, a sewing machine with mechanical problems is a frustrating obstacle to creativity. In the beginning of my quiltmaking career, I bought an inexpensive machine. I couldn't sew for more than ten minutes without something going wrong. I thought my sewing skills were hopeless. Fortunately, a friend let me try her machine and I realized the problems I was having weren't my fault. Needless to say, I purchased a better sewing machine.

◆ Always use a fine-point permanent ink pen or a chalk-wheel device for marking the cutting lines on fabric. The thinner the line, the more accurate the pattern pieces will be. So no dull pencils, please. They are a definite no-no!

◆ You should have two clear plastic rulers: 6" x 24" and a smaller 2" x 18". You also need a retractable metal or cloth tape measure for determining the width and length of a quilt top.

◆ I couldn't design a quilt without the help of a reducing glass. This handy-dandy little tool looks like a magnifying glass, but instead of enlarging an image, it makes it appear farther away. When you study your developing quilt top through a reducing glass, design errors in color and value become obvious.

◆ The only other items you'll need to make the patterns in this book are: a sheet of template plastic, a few spools of cotton thread, your batting of choice, and some good quality pins: both straight and safety.

◆ Oh yes, you will also need a little patience, a willing spirit, and an abiding desire to put more fabrics into your quilts than you ever dreamed possible. I know you're going to love the results!

The Log Cabin is an *American classic* and no other quilt pattern is quite so reminiscent of our forefathers' quest for adventure and homesteading. As pioneer families traveled west and settled the new frontiers, men built log cabins with lumber and mud and the women built them with fabric and thread.

Both the builder and quiltmaker started with a sturdy foundation. Stones, secured with clay, were topped with logs (layered in an interlocking pattern) to form the cabin. A similar procedure was used to make a log cabin quilt. Instead of sewing one piece of fabric to another, as in conventional patchwork, the log cabin quilt block was worked on its own foundation, usually a piece of muslin (eliminating the need for batting). Scraps of old blankets and worn-out clothing were cut into strips and sewn around a center square. Whenever possible, the square was made with a bright red or yellow fabric to represent the hearth of the home. When the blocks were sewn together, they could be quickly tied to a heavy backing material and used on cabin walls and beds for protection against cold and snowy winters.

Anatomy of the Log Cabin Block

The basic Log Cabin block is a square that is visually divided by a light and dark triangle. Depending on how the blocks are sewn together, various patterns emerge. Streak of Lightning, Straight Furrows, and Barn Raising are just a few of the colorfully named settings.

In my opinion, the best Log Cabin quilts have a feeling of unity between the lighter and darker areas—almost as if the same fabrics are used on both sides of the center square and a real shadow is being cast across the surface. This illusion is easily achieved. First, decide on your color scheme. Then select some lighter- and darker-colored fabrics in each of those hues. Also select a few mediums to use on both sides of the center square. This will give the block more interest and reinforce the sunshine and shadow effect.

PAINTED
SHADOWS

Painted Shadows, 26½" x 31½" (size before quilting), Gai Perry

PAINTED SHADOWS

The *Painted Shadows* quilt is set in the Straight Furrows pattern. It can be made bigger by adding additional blocks or by making the log strips wider and the center squares larger. It can also be made with prints instead of solids—or try a combination of both. Although the early Log Cabin blocks were sewn to a foundation, I have omitted this step. The result is a lighter-weight quilt that will hang on the wall more gracefully.

Color and Fabric Suggestions

It's impossible to put too many fabrics into a Log Cabin quilt. The more, the merrier! *Painted Shadows* was made with a range of light, medium, and dark solid-colored fabrics. The vivid combination of red, brick, plum, blue, green, olive, teal, mustard, tan, and black produced a quilt that resembles a piece of vintage folk art.

Begin by gathering some light, medium, and dark solid-colored fabrics in the hues listed above or develop your own color scheme using at least three Color Families. (Refer to page 8 for a description of Color Families.) This might be a challenge, but give it a try. Make sure that each of the colors has a variety of tints, tones, and shades because using different interpretations of a color is infinitely more interesting than repeating the same one over and over again.

5" finished Log Cabin block

Fabric Quantities

This is definitely a scrap quilt and only a small quantity of each fabric is needed. Pull from your stash, then beg, borrow, and buy whatever your conscience will allow. Purchase ⅛-yard pieces for the log strips. That way, you can get eight different fabrics for the price of a yard.

Blocks and Pieced Border
Light, Medium, and Dark Solids (including black): ⅛ yard each (or scraps) of approximately 24 fabrics. (You will use approximately 10 lights, 10 darks, and 4 mediums.)
Bright Solid: ⅛ yard for center squares.
Inner Border
¼ yard dark solid
Backing: 1 yard
Binding: ⅜ yard light solid
Batting: 30" x 35"

Cutting
Strips are cut crosswise unless otherwise noted.

Blocks
You will need 20 blocks.
Light, Medium, and Dark Solids
◆ Cut into strips 1" wide. You will need enough for 20 blocks and the strip-pieced border. Don't worry about running out of a particular fabric because when you do, just substitute another one.
Bright Solid
◆ Cut 1 strip 1½" wide, then cut into 20 squares 1½" x 1½".

Inner Border
Dark Solid
◆ Cut 4 strips 1½" wide.

Designing the Blocks

Sort the strips into lights, mediums, and darks and begin stitching the blocks. Make an effort to put a combination of warm and cool colors into each block and try not to make any two blocks exactly alike. Also, remember to use some colors in the medium-value range on either side of the center square. As you sew the blocks, put them on a design wall or board and critique your work.

Block Construction

1. Sew the first lighter-colored strip to the center square. Finger-press and trim.

2. Rotate the block a quarter turn and sew more of the same strip to the center square. Finger-press and trim.

3. Rotate the block another a quarter turn and sew the first darker-colored strip to the center square. Finger-press the strip away from the square and trim even.

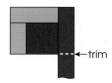

4. Rotate the block another a quarter turn and sew more of the same strip it to the center square. Finger-press and trim.

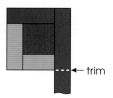

5. Rotate the block another a quarter turn and sew a second lighter-colored strip to the block above the first lighter-colored log. Finger-press and trim. Continue adding strips in the same manner until there are 4 lighter- and 4 darker-colored logs on each side of the center square.

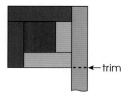

Quilt Top Construction

1. Referring to the diagram on page 16 and the quilt photo on page 13, arrange the blocks. Start at the bottom and use the One-Pin, Two-Pin Sewing Method, pages 115–117, to sew each row of blocks together. Alternate the pressing direction of the seams from row to row.

2. Join the rows and press the seams in one direction.

Borders

1. Turn to Sewing Essentials, pages 117–118, for information on measuring and attaching borders.

2. Trim the inner border strips to the appropriate lengths and sew them to the quilt top.

3. Sew the leftover 1"-wide log strips together in groups of five. Cut into 2½" segments. Sew these segments together until you have 2 borders for the sides and 2 borders for the top and bottom that fit the quilt's measurements. Sew to the quilt top. Press the seams toward the inner border.

Finishing

Turn to Sewing Essentials, page 119–121, for finishing instructions.

Suggested Quilting

When I photographed my quilt top, I thought it looked painted rather than sewn so I decided to encourage the illusion. I used flannel for the batting and did some invisible-tacking instead of quilting. To make an invisible-tack, make 2–3 tiny stitches in the well of the seam. This is just one of many approaches, and I encourage you to use your imagination when choosing a quilting solution for your Log Cabin quilt.

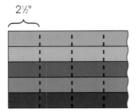

2½"

Sew log strips and cut into 2½" segments.

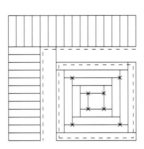

Suggested Quilting Pattern; x indicates an invisible-tack.

Painted Shadows Design & Construction Guide

A GATHERING
OF RAINBOWS

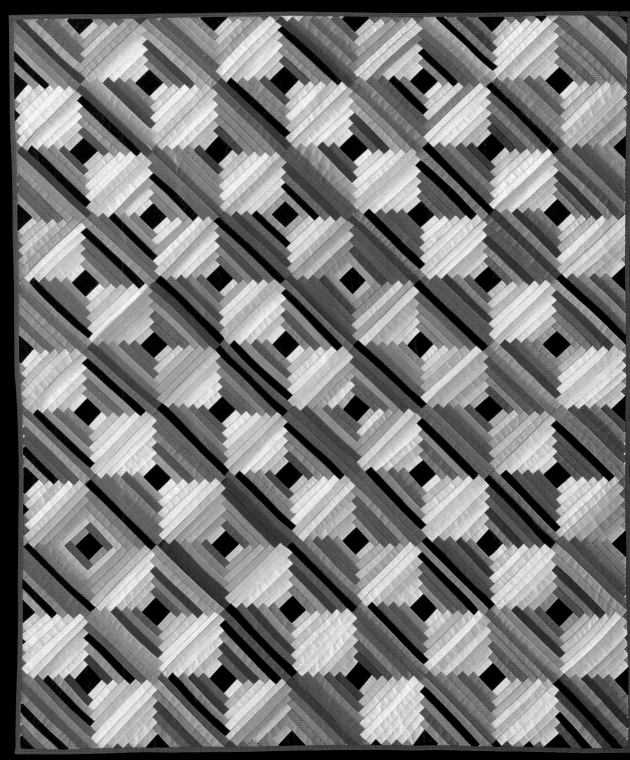

A Gathering of Rainbows, 40½" x 49" (size before quilting), Gai Perry

The Court House Steps block is one of several Log Cabin variations. The center black square is said to represent a judge's robe and the surrounding logs are the steps of the judicial system. *A Gathering of Rainbows* was made with a full spectrum (six Color Families) of solid-colored fabrics. In my mind's eye, I see it as a pastel quilt, but in reality, many of the colors are surprisingly intense. For the lighter areas, look for creamy tints of pistachio, peach, avocado, lemon, lavender, blueberry, peacock, watermelon, ecru, and mocha. For the darker areas, find deeper tones of the above colors, plus grape and black.

To make a larger quilt, increase the width of the logs and the size of the center squares.

6¼" finished Court House Steps block

Fabric Quantities

Work with the colors mentioned above or develop your own variation of the color scheme.

Blocks

Light, Medium, and Dark Solids (including black): ¼ yard each (or scraps) of approximately 24 fabrics

Black Solid: ¼ yard for center squares

Backing: 2½ yards

Binding: ⅓ yard dark solid

Batting: 44" x 53"

Template plastic

Cutting

Strips are cut crosswise unless otherwise noted.

Blocks

You will need 60 blocks.

Light, Medium, and Dark Solids

◆ Cut into strips 1" wide.

Black Solid

◆ Cut 3 strips 1¾" wide, then cut into 60 squares 1¾" x 1¾".

Designing the Blocks

Sort the strips into lights, mediums, and darks. Make an effort to combine warm and cool colors in each block and try not to make any two blocks exactly alike. Occasionally, use some colors from the medium-value range within the darker and lighter areas. As you sew the blocks, put them on your design wall or board and critique. Note: Twenty of the sixty blocks will eventually be cut into triangles to go around the perimeter of the quilt.

Block Construction

1. Sew the first lighter-colored strip to the center square. Finger-press the strip away from the square and trim even with the center square. Sew more of the same strip to the opposite side of the center square. Finger-press the strip away from the square and trim even.

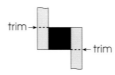

2. Rotate the block and sew the first darker-colored strip to the center square. Finger-press the strip away from the square and trim even. Sew more of the same strip to the opposite side of the center square. Finger press the strip away from the square and trim even.

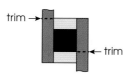

trim → ← trim

3. Rotate the block and sew a second lighter-colored strip to the block above the first lighter-colored log. Finger-press the strip away from the square and trim even. Continue adding strips in this manner until there are 5 lighter- and 5 darker-colored strips stitched around the center square. Make 60 blocks.

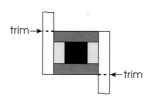

trim → ← trim

Perimeter Triangles

In order to place the Court House Steps blocks on point, you will need to cut 18 blocks into perimeter triangles and 2 blocks into corner triangles. Refer to the cutting perimeter triangles diagrams shown below. The template pattern for the two corner triangles is on page 20. (Maybe you can think of something clever to do with the unusable sections.)

1. To make the side perimeter triangles, place a block on your cutting mat with the *lighter strips* appearing on the lower left side. Position a clear plastic ruler so that the top edge of the ruler is touching the east and west points of

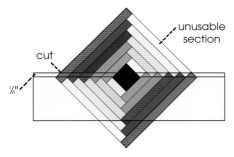

the block. Now move the ruler up ¼" and with your rotary cutter, cut the block along the top edge of the ruler. (Set aside the unusable upper section.) Make a total of 10.

2. To make the top and bottom perimeter triangles, place a block on your cutting mat with the *darker strips* appearing on the lower left side. Position a clear plastic ruler so that the top edge of the ruler is touching the east and west points of the block. Now move the ruler up ¼" and cut the block along the top edge of the ruler. Set aside the unusable upper section. Make a total of 8.

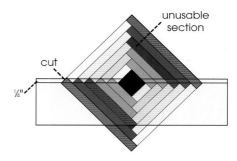

3. Make a plastic template using the Corner Triangle pattern on page 20. If necessary, refer to Making and Using Templates on page 115. Position the template over the darker strips of a block with the point of the triangle covering part of the center square. Cut the block and set aside the unusable upper section. Cut 2 blocks in this manner.

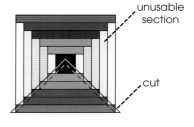

Quilt Top Construction

1. Referring to the diagram below and the quilt photo on page 17, arrange the blocks and the perimeter and corner triangles.

2. Start at the lower left corner and use the One-Pin, Two-Pin Sewing Method, pages 115–117, to sew the blocks into diagonal rows. Alternate the pressing direction of the seams from row to row.

3. Sew the rows together and press all the seams in one direction.

A Gathering of Rainbows Design & Construction Guide

Finishing

Turn to Sewing Essentials, pages 119–121, for finishing instructions.

Suggested Quilting

I liked the unquilted look of *Painted Shadows* so I applied the same technique to this quilt. I used flannel instead of batting, and did some invisible tacking instead of quilting. To make an invisible-tack, make 2–3 tiny stitches in the well of the seam.

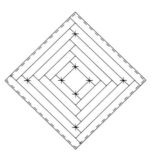

Suggested Quilting Pattern; x indicates an invisible-tack.

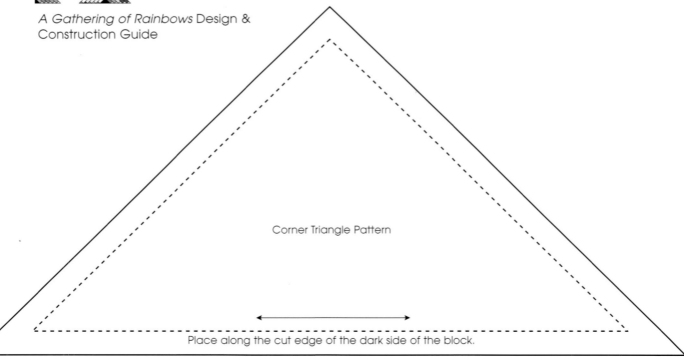

Corner Triangle Pattern

Place along the cut edge of the dark side of the block.

KALEIDOSCOPES

Kaleidoscope, known as an "optical illusion" or fool-the-eye quilt pattern, is intriguing because the individual block construction is so simple—just eight wedge-shaped pieces and four corner triangles. Who could guess that when several of these blocks are sewn together, a shape-shifting marvel of overlapping circles and pinwheels would emerge?

Some of the most wonderful antique kaleidoscope quilts are made with scraps. I know that I've said this before, but it's worth repeating. It is easier to put fifty different fabrics into a quilt than it is to choose five that work brilliantly together. The logic is that when dozens of fabrics are involved, a few *clinkers* won't be noticed. With just five fabrics, if one of them is inappropriate, the whole quilt is affected.

Anatomy of the Kaleidoscope Block

The Kaleidoscope block has only twelve pieces so you may wonder how it can create such optical magic. The method couldn't be easier! All you have to do is alternate lighter- and darker-colored prints for the wedge-shaped pieces and use *very light* prints for the four corner triangles.

MIRACLES
AND WONDERS

Miracles and Wonders, 54½" x 61½" (size before quilting), Gai Perry

This traditional style quilt has the look of a mellow old antique. It was made with fabrics that are reminiscent of prints that have been available for a hundred years.

Color and Fabric Suggestions

Miracles and Wonders contains a broad range of colors including lighter- and darker-colored prints from the Red, Yellow, Blue, and Green Color Families. The corner triangles were made with very light prints in tints of pink, blue, green, and cream. Fabric patterns include plaids, stripes, polka dots, tiny florals, and geometrics. In other words—anything goes!

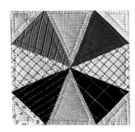

7" finished Kaleidoscope block

Fabric Quantities

Use suggested colors or create your own interpretation of the color scheme.

Blocks

Lighter-Colored Fabrics: ¼ yard each of at least 20 fabrics, plus additional scraps

Darker-Colored Fabrics: ¼ yard each of at least 20 fabrics, plus additional scraps. (Choose fabrics in the same hues as the lighter fabrics, but in darker values.)

Very Light-Colored Fabrics: ⅛ yard each of 8–12 fabrics in the same colors as above, but even lighter for the corner triangles, plus additional scraps. Note: Use the reverse sides of some of the lighter fabrics to help fill this category.

Border

1⅔ yards (You can get by with ⅝ yard if you're willing to cut the borders crosswise and do some piecing.)

Binding: ½ yard

Backing: 3⅓ yards

Batting: 58" x 65"

Template plastic

Cutting

Blocks

Make a plastic template of the pattern for the 7" Kaleidoscope block on page 25. If necessary, refer to Making and Using Templates on page 115. Use the template to cut the following pieces for each block. Refer to Designing the Blocks on page 24 before cutting fabrics, then start cutting and designing a few blocks at a time. You will need 56 blocks.

Lighter-Colored Fabrics

◆ Cut 4 for each block. (You will need 224 total.)

Darker-Colored Fabrics

◆ Cut 4 for each block. (You will need 224 total.)

Very Light-Colored Fabrics

Note: Don't cut corner triangles yet. They will be added after the blocks are partially sewn.

Border

◆ Cut 4 lengthwise strips 3" x 58" or cut 6 crosswise strips 3" wide.

Designing the Blocks

Design each octagonal section of the block as though it were a complete little quilt and use the following kinds of contrasts.

1. Contrast of small-, medium-, and large-scale prints.
2. Contrast of print style (stripes, plaids, florals, geometrics, etc.).
3. Contrast of warm and cool colors.

Design note: Resist making a block with lighter and darker values of the same color.

Take a moment to study the *Miracles and Wonders* quilt on page 22. Notice that some blocks have as few as two or three different fabrics while others have as many as six or seven. Try working with the following fabric combinations for the first seven blocks. It should give you a real understanding of the "scrap" concept.

Block One 1 lighter-colored print and
    1 darker-colored fabric

Block Two 2 lighter-colored prints and
    1 darker-colored fabric

Block Three 3 lighter-colored prints and
    1 darker-colored fabric

Block Four 1 lighter-colored print and
    2 darker-colored fabrics

Block Five 1 lighter-colored print and
    3 darker-colored fabrics

Block Six 2 lighter-colored prints and
    2 darker-colored fabrics

Block Seven 3 lighter-colored prints and
    3 darker-colored fabrics

When you have designed several blocks (minus the corner triangles) and like the way they look, start sewing. Continue designing and sewing until the 56 blocks are partially assembled.

Block Construction

1. Sew 4 pairs of lighter- and darker-colored wedge-shaped pieces. Press in the direction of the arrows.

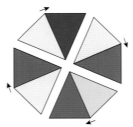

2. Sew 2 sets of 2 pairs. Press in the direction of the arrows.

3. Sew the 2 sets of pairs together. Press the seam open.

Quilt Top Construction

1. Referring to the diagram on page 25 and the quilt photo on page 22, arrange the blocks. Rotate each block so a darker-colored wedge-shaped piece opposes a lighter-colored wedge-shaped piece in the adjoining block.

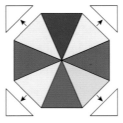

2. When you have placed each block exactly where it is going to be sewn, add the corner tri-

angles. Cut 112 squares 3" x 3" from the very light fabrics. Cut each of the squares diagonally in half for a total of 224 triangles. Stitch 4 triangles to the corners of each block. Press.

Design Note: The corners are added last to ensure that there are four different very light-colored triangles where the block corners converge.

3. Start at the bottom and use the One-Pin, Two-Pin Sewing Method, pages 115–117, to sew each row of blocks together. Alternate the pressing direction of the seams from row to row. Sew the rows together and press all the seams in one direction.

Border

1. Turn to Sewing Essentials, pages 117–118, for information on measuring and attaching borders.

2. Piece the strips together, if necessary, and trim the border strips to the appropriate lengths. Sew them to the quilt top. Press the seams toward the border.

Finishing

Turn to Sewing Essentials, pages 119–121, for finishing instructions.

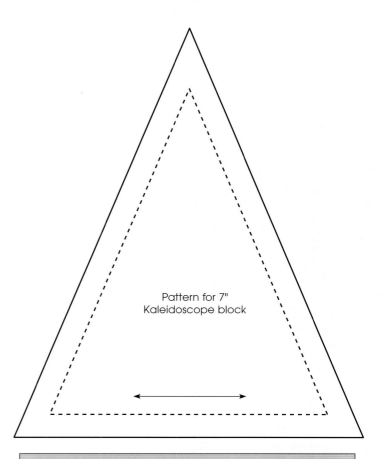

Pattern for 7" Kaleidoscope block

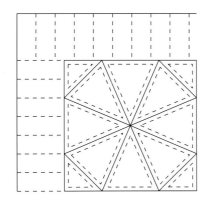

Suggested Quilting Pattern

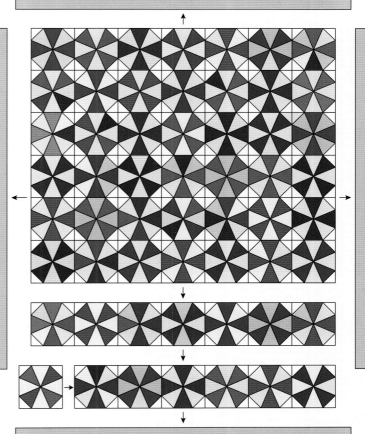

Miracles and Wonders Design & Construction Guide

Cool Circles, 41" x 47

*C*ool Circles was made with a 6"
Kaleidoscope block and is one row
narrower in width and length. The
Green and Blue Color Families were used to
create the striking analo-
gous color scheme. (See
page 9 for an explana-
tion of analogous.) The
use of contemporary
fabrics gives the quilt a
modern appearance.

6" finished
Kaleidoscope block

Fabric Quantities

Work with the Color Families and fabric
styles mentioned above or create your own
analogous color scheme.

Blocks

Lighter-Colored Fabrics: ⅛ yard each of at
    least 20 fabrics, plus additional scraps
Darker-Colored Fabrics: ⅛ yard each of at least
    20 fabrics, plus additional scraps, in the
    same hues as the lighter-colored fabrics, but
    in darker values
Very Light-Colored Fabrics: ⅛ yard each of 8–12
    prints, plus additional scraps, in the same
    colors as above, but even lighter for corner
    triangles. Use the reverse sides of some of the
    lighter prints to help fill this category.

Borders and Binding

Inner Border: ¼ yard light solid
Outer Border and Binding: 1⅜ yards dark
    solid. (You can get by with ⅔ yard if you're
    willing to cut the borders crosswise and do
    some piecing.)
Backing: 2½ yards
Batting: 45" x 51"
Template plastic

Cutting

*Strips are cut crosswise unless otherwise
noted.*

Blocks

*Make a plastic template of the pattern for
the 6" Kaleidoscope block on page 29. If necessary, refer to Making and Using Templates on
page 115. Use the template to cut the following
pieces for each block. Refer to Designing the
Blocks on page 24 before cutting fabrics, then
start cutting and designing a few blocks at a
time. You will need 42 blocks.*

Lighter-Colored Fabrics
◆ Cut 4 for each block. (You will need 168
    total.)
Darker-Colored Fabrics
◆ Cut 4 for each block. (You will need 168
    total.)
Very Light-Colored Fabrics
    Note: Don't cut corner triangles yet. They
will be added after the blocks are partially
sewn.

Borders

Inner Border
◆ Cut 4 strips 1" wide. Depending on the
    width of your fabric, you may need to cut
    an additional strip and piece strips together.
Outer Border
◆ Cut 4 lengthwise strips 2¼" x approximately
    46" or 5 crosswise strips 2¼" wide.

Designing the Blocks

Make 42 blocks (minus corner triangles).

COOL CIRCLES

Block Construction

1. Sew 4 pairs of lighter- and darker-colored wedged-shaped pieces. Press in the direction of the arrows.

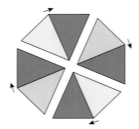

2. Sew 2 sets of 2 pairs. Press in the direction of the arrows.

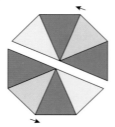

3. Sew the 2 sets of pairs together. Press the seam open.

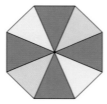

Quilt Top Construction

1. Refer to the *Cool Circles* Design & Construction Guide on page 29 and the quilt photo on page 26 as a reference to arrange the blocks. Rotate each block so a darker-colored wedge-shaped piece opposes a lighter-colored wedge-shaped piece in the adjoining block.

2. When you have placed each block exactly where it is going to be sewn, add the corner tri-angles. Cut 84 squares 2⅝" x 2⅝" from the light-est fabrics. Cut each of the squares diagonally in half for a total of 168 triangles. Stitch the triangles to the four corners of each block. Press.

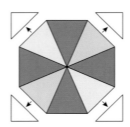

Design Note: The corners are added last to ensure that there are four different very light-colored triangles where the block corners converge.

3. Start at the bottom and use the One-Pin, Two-Pin Sewing Method, pages 115–117, to sew each row of blocks together. Alternate the pressing direction of the seams from row to row. Sew the rows together and press all the seams in one direction.

Borders

1. Turn to Sewing Essentials, pages 117–118, for information on measuring and attaching borders.

2. Piece the strips together, if necessary, and trim inner border strips to the appropriate lengths. Sew them to the quilt top. Press the seams toward the border.

3. Add the outer borders in the same manner.

Finishing

Turn to Sewing Essentials, pages 119–121, for finishing instructions.

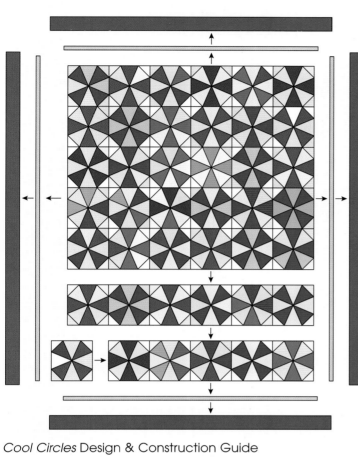

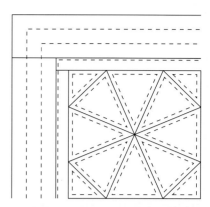

Suggested Quilting Pattern

Cool Circles Design & Construction Guide

Mini Miracles, Framed Size: 26" x 30",
Gai Perry. This quilt was made with
6" Kaleidoscope blocks.

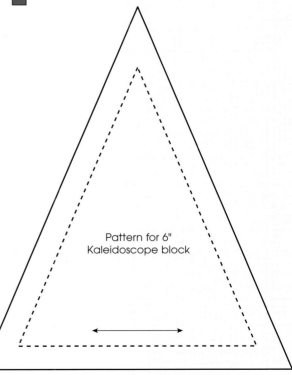

Pattern for 6"
Kaleidoscope block

BASKETS

I grew up with a mother who could have been a character in an F. Scott Fitzgerald novel. Whenever I caught her doing something silly or even slightly undignified, she always laughed and said, "Do what I say, not what I do." This double standard annoyed me but I forgave her because she was so much fun.

Just before I was married, she presented me with some charmingly quaint advice. She told me that I should always decorate the master bedroom in an intimate and romantic fashion so my husband would feel as though he was entering a *boudoir*— and the effect would be stimulating.

Decades later I still smile when I remember her well-intentioned advice, and since *Victorian Country Baskets* is probably the most romantic looking quilt I'll ever make, its hangs in our bedroom. Thanks, Mom!

Anatomy of the Flower Basket Block

There must be dozens of basket block variations. Some have baskets containing flowers (interpreted with triangles), while others are empty, but have stylish handles or fancy trims. The first quilt in this section was made with a traditional Flower Basket block. It's an uncomplicated design with relatively few pattern pieces. It requires only one darker-colored print for the basket and flower triangles and a second, lighter-colored print for the background area.

VICTORIAN
COUNTRY BASKETS

Victorian Country Baskets, 60½" x 60½" (size before quilting), Gai Perry

VICTORIAN COUNTRY BASKETS

This quilt is all about flowers! Large, chintz-style flowers and dainty calicos combine to create a garden of opulent blooms. The personality of the fabrics is Victorian, but the basket design is pure country.

Color and Fabric Suggestions

Each of the 16 blocks contains 2 fabrics; a black background print for the basket and flower triangles and a pink, cream, white, or turquoise print for the background. The alternate squares feature a large-scale, cream and rose floral print. The perimeter triangles are an elegant red-violet, damask-textured print, and the border combines a lavender stripe with yet another large-scale floral print.

8" finished Flower Basket block (variation)

Fabric Quantities

Work with the colors and fabric styles mentioned above or develop your own variation of the color scheme.

Blocks

Floral Fabrics with Dark Backgrounds:
  12" x 12" scraps of 16 different fabrics for baskets and flower triangles

Floral Fabrics with Light Backgrounds:
  12" x 12" scraps of 16 different fabrics for block backgrounds

Alternate Blocks

Large-Scale Light Floral Print: ¾ yard

Perimeter Triangles

Medium-Dark, Textured Print: ⅝ yard

Borders

Inner Border: ⅝ yard striped print

Outer Border: 1¾ yards of a large-scale, dark background floral print. (You can get by with 1⅛ yards if you are willing to cut borders crosswise and do some piecing.)

Binding: ⅝ yard of dark solid

Backing: 3⅝ yards

Batting: 64" x 64"

Cutting

Strips are cut crosswise unless otherwise noted.

Blocks

Refer to the Flower Basket Block Sewing Guide on page 33 and cut the following pieces for each block. The cutting method ensures a straight grain is stitched to a bias grain to prevent stretching. You will need 16 blocks.

Floral Fabrics with Dark Backgrounds

◆ Cut 1 square 6⅞" x 6⅞", then cut diagonally in half to make 2 triangles (A). (You will not use 1 triangle.)

◆ Cut 2 squares (4⅛" x 4⅛"), then cut diagonally in half in both directions to make 8 triangles (B). (You will not use 3 triangles.)

Floral Fabrics with Light Backgrounds

◆ Cut 3 squares 2⅞" x 2⅞", then cut diagonally in half to make 6 triangles (C).

◆ Cut 2 rectangles 2½" x 4½" (D).

◆ Cut 1 square 4⅞" x 4⅞", then cut diagonally in half to make 2 triangles (E). (You will not use 1 triangle.)

Alternate Squares

Large-Scale Light Floral Print

◆ Cut 3 strips 8½" wide, then cut into 9 squares 8½" x 8½" for alternate squares.

Perimeter Triangles

Medium-Dark Textured Print

◆ Cut 3 squares 12⅝" x 12⅝", then cut diagonally in half in both directions to make 12 side perimeter triangles.

◆ Cut 2 squares 6⅝" x 6⅝", then cut diagonally in half to make 4 corner perimeter triangles.

Borders

Inner Border

◆ Cut 5 strips 2¾" wide.

Outer Border

◆ Cut 2 lengthwise strips 5½" x 52" and 2 lengthwise strips 5½" x 62".

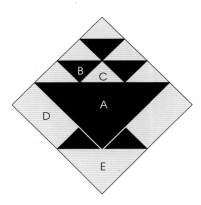

Flower Basket Block

Designing the Block

Design 16 blocks. As you cut the pattern pieces for each block, arrange them on your design wall or board and decide if you have achieved an attractive contrast of print scale and value. Keep rearranging until you are satisfied.

Block Construction

1. To make Unit 1, sew 3 B and C triangles into squares. Press toward the darker triangles and clip off the ears. Sew the squares together and attach the 3 remaining C triangles into rows as shown. Press in the direction of the arrows. Sew the rows together. Press seams in one direction.

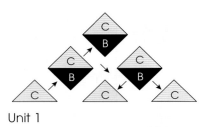

Unit 1

2. To make Unit 2, sew the 2 B triangles to the 2 D rectangles. Press in the direction of the arrows. Sew the B/D units to the large A triangle. Press. Attach the E triangle. Press.

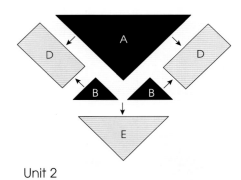

Unit 2

3. Join Units 1 and 2. Press toward Unit 2.

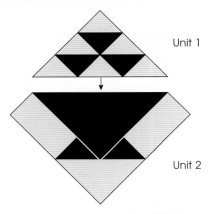

Flower Basket Block Sewing Guide

Quilt Top Construction

1. Arrange the basket blocks, the alternate squares, and the perimeter triangles in diagonal rows as shown in the *Victorian Country Baskets* Design & Construction Guide.

2. Start at the lower left-hand corner and use the One-Pin, Two-Pin Sewing Method, pages 115–117, to sew diagonal rows of basket blocks, alternate squares, and perimeter triangles. Press the seams toward the alternate blocks and perimeter triangles. Join the rows and press all the seams in one direction.

Borders

1. Turn to Sewing Essentials, pages 117–118, for information on measuring and attaching borders.

2. Piece, if necessary, and trim the inner border strips to the appropriate length. Sew them to the quilt top. Press seams toward the border.

3. Add the outer borders in the same manner.

Finishing

Turn to Sewing Essentials, pages 119–121, for finishing information.

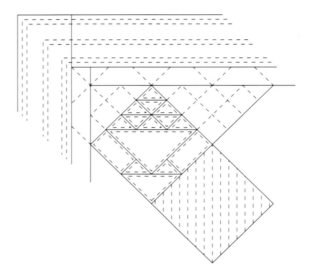

Suggested Quilting Pattern

Victorian Country Baskets Design & Construction Guide

A TISKET, A TASKET,
I'VE GOT AN EXTRA BASKET!

A Tisket A Tasket, I've Got An Extra Basket!, 61¼" x 48¼" (size before quilting), Gai Perry

I designed an oversize block using lots of small squares for the basket motif. My original idea was to make nine basket blocks that were packed with bright colors and use a dull-colored print for the alternate squares. I was hoping the contrast of opposites would be exciting—but it wasn't. I needed a livelier print for the alternate squares. I hunted high and low but couldn't find what I wanted so the blocks were put on a back burner.

Two years later, I found a yellow floral I thought would be perfect for the alternate squares—but it wasn't. Too much yellow! My final solution was to butt the squares together and use a solid black for the perimeter triangles. But wait a minute. There was an extra block. Oh, no! After this much effort, nothing was going to be wasted. *A-Tisket A-Tasket, I've Got An Extra Basket* is the result and I finally got lucky because the yellow floral print made a terrific border.

12" finished *A-Tisket, A-Tasket, I've Got An Extra Basket* block

Fabric Quantities

This isn't a color scheme for the faint-of-heart so if your comfort level leans toward a more subdued palette, make substitutions.

Blocks

Colorful Scraps: Dozens measuring at least 2" square in an assortment of light, medium, and dark-bright prints to total approximately 1 yard for baskets

Dark Solid: 1¾ yards for basket backgrounds, perimeter triangles, and basket handles

Brightly-Colored Print: 1⅛ yards for block backgrounds

Border

Light, Large-Scale Floral Print: 1½ yards

Binding: ½ yard

Backing: 3 yards

Batting: 66" x 53"

Cutting

Strips are cut crosswise unless otherwise noted.

Blocks

Cut the following pieces for each block. You will need 9 blocks.

Colorful Scraps

◆ Cut 27 squares 1½" x 1½" (A). (Note: Use only 2 or 3 of the prints more than once in each block.)

Dark Solid

◆ Cut 20 squares 1½" x 1½" (B).
◆ Cut 1 rectangle 1½" x 7½" (C).
◆ Cut 1 rectangle 1½" x 6½" (D).
◆ Cut 8 squares 1⅞" x 1⅞", then cut diagonally in half to make 16 triangles (E). (Note: Two of them will be sewn to the basket handles.)

Brightly-Colored Print

◆ Cut 1 square 4⅞" x 4⅞", then cut in half diagonally to make 2 triangles (F). (Save the extra for another block.)
◆ Cut 2 rectangles 2½" x 8½" (G).
◆ Cut 1 square 6⅞" x 6⅞", then cut in half diagonally to make 2 triangles (H). (Save the extra for another block.)

- Cut 1 rectangle 1½" x 9½" (I).
- Cut 1 rectangle 1½" x 8½" (J).
- Cut 1 square 1⅞" x 1⅞", then cut diagonally in half to make 2 triangles (K).

Perimeter Triangles

Dark Solid

- Cut 2 squares 18¼" x 18¼", then cut diagonally in half in both directions to make 8 side perimeter triangles. (You will not use 3 triangles.)
- Cut 2 squares 9⅜" x 9⅜", then cut in half diagonally to make 4 corner perimeter triangles.

Border

Light, Large-Scale Floral Print

- Cut 4 strips 5½" wide.
- Cut 2 strips 9½" wide.

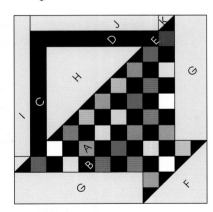

A-Tisket, A-Tasket, I've Got An Extra Basket Block Sewing Guide

Designing the Blocks

Arrange all the pieces for the first block on your design wall or board. Now stand back and decide if the assortment of small print squares is strong enough to balance the intensity of the bright background print. If not, make substitutions. When you are satisfied with the first block, sew it using the *A-Tisket, A-Tasket, I've Got An Extra Basket* Block Sewing Guide as a reference. Make 8 more blocks using a different arrangement of colored squares for each block.

Block Construction

1. To make Unit 1, sew the 2 E triangles to the C and D basket handles. Press in the direction of the arrows. Sew C/E and D/E to the H triangle. Press. Sew the K triangles to the I and J background rectangles. Press. Sew the I/K and J/K units to the basket handles. Press.

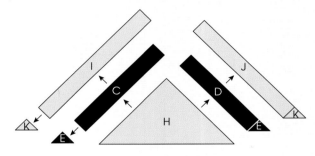

Unit 1

2. To make Unit 2, sew diagonal rows of A and B squares and E triangles. Press the seams in opposite directions. Join the rows and press all the seams in one direction. Sew an E triangle to each side of 2 A squares. Press. Sew A/E units to

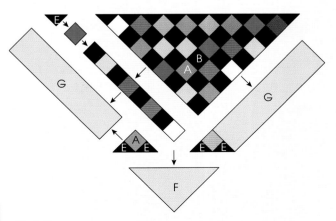

Unit 2

each of the 2 G rectangles. Press. Sew
A/E/G units to the basket. Press.
Attach triangle F. Press.

3. Join Units 1 and 2. Press the
seams toward Unit 1.

Quilt Top Construction

1. Arrange the sewn blocks and the
perimeter triangles as shown on the
*A-Tisket, A-Tasket I've Got An
Extra Basket* Design &
Construction Guide.

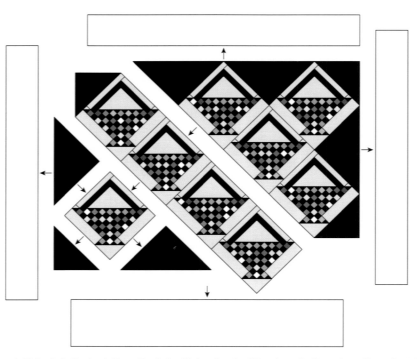

2. Start at the lower left-hand corner
and use the One-Pin, Two-Pin Sewing Method,
pages 115–117, to sew diagonal rows of baskets
and perimeter triangles. Alternate the pressing
direction of the seams from row to row.

3. Sew the rows together and press all the
seams in one direction. Note: The bottom of
the basket block at the lower end of the second
diagonal row will eventually be appliquéd to
the border.

Border

Turn to Sewing Essentials, pages 117–118, for
information on measuring and attaching borders.

1. Piece, if necessary, and trim the border strips
to the appropriate lengths. Sew the top and
bottom borders and then the side borders to
the quilt top. Press seams toward the border.

2. Turn ¼" under on the exposed edges of the
lower basket. Using your favorite method,
appliqué the edges to the border.

A-Tisket, A-Tasket, I've Got An Extra Basket Design & Construction Guide

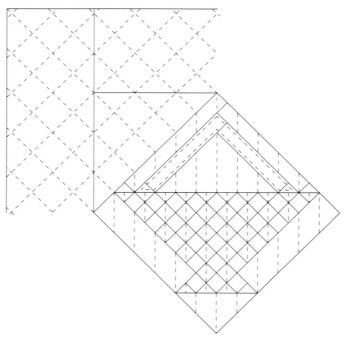

Suggested Quilting Pattern

Finishing

Turn to Sewing Essentials, pages 119–121,
for finishing information. On a whim, I put a
wider-than-average binding on this quilt, but a
standard-size binding is perfectly acceptable.

VINTAGE
SCRAP BASKETS

Vintage Scrap Baskets, 66½" x 78" (size before quilting), Gai Perry. Machine quilted by Karen Nelson.

VINTAGE SCRAP BASKETS

With all the gorgeous collections of museum-reproduction fabrics available, it's a breeze to make a quilt that looks like a family heirloom. A crewel border print inspired the color scheme for *Vintage Scrap Baskets*. The baskets were made with several coordinating prints from the same collection plus additional prints from my stash.

Each of the blocks has one lighter-colored print and one darker-colored print. As you select fabrics, try to maintain the integrity of the quilt's vintage appearance. That means—no batiks or contemporary-looking fabrics!

8" finished Flower Basket block (variation)

Fabric Quantities

The museum-reproduction print you select for the border will act as a *focus fabric* and dictate the color scheme. Approximately 22 different combinations of lighter- and darker-colored prints were used to make the 32 basket blocks. You may elect to use less—or more.

Blocks

Lighter-Colored Prints: Baskets and
  Backgrounds: 12" x 15" scraps of 20 different fabrics for the lighter-colored baskets and backgrounds, approximately 3 yards total

Darker-Colored Prints: 12" x 15" scraps of 20 different fabrics for the darker-colored baskets and backgrounds, approximately 3 yards total

Perimeter Triangles

Darker-Colored Print: 1 yard

Borders

Inner Border: ⅜ yard light solid

Middle Border: 2⅜ yards companion print to the outer border

Outer Border: 2⅜ yards large-scale museum-reproduction print. (Note: You can get by with less border yardage if you are willing to do some piecing.)

Binding: ½ yard of a darker-colored print

Backing: 4 yards

Batting: 70" x 82"

Cutting

Strips are cut crosswise unless otherwise noted.

Blocks

Refer to the Flower Basket Block Sewing Guide, page 42, and cut the following pieces for each block. The cutting method ensures a straight grain is stitched to a bias grain to prevent stretching. You will need 12 Basket blocks that have lighter backgrounds and 20 that have darker backgrounds.

For each of the 12 blocks with lighter backgrounds:

Darker-Colored Prints

◆ Cut 1 square 4⅞" x 4⅞", then cut diagonally in half for triangle (A).

◆ Cut 2 squares 4¼" x 4¼", then cut diagonally in half in both directions for 8 triangles (B).

Lighter-Colored Prints

◆ Cut 4 squares 2⅞" x 2⅞", then cut diagonally in half for 8 triangles (C).

◆ Cut 2 rectangles 2½" x 4½" (D).

◆ Cut 1 square 4⅞" x 4⅞", then cut diagonally in half for triangle (E).

For each of the 20 blocks with darker backgrounds:

Darker-Colored Prints
◆ Cut 4 squares 2⅞" x 2⅞", then cut diagonally in half for 8 triangles (C).
◆ Cut 2 rectangles 2½" x 4½" (D).
◆ Cut 1 square 4⅞" x 4⅞", then cut diagonally in half for triangle (E).

Lighter-Colored Prints
◆ Cut 1 square 4⅞" x 4⅞", then cut diagonally in half for triangle (A).
◆ Cut 2 squares 4¼" x 4¼", then cut diagonally in half in both directions for 8 triangles (B).

Perimeter Triangles

Darker-Colored Print
◆ Cut 4 squares 12⅝" x 12⅝", then cut diagonally in half in both directions for side perimeter triangles. (There will be 2 extra triangles.)
◆ Cut 2 squares 6⅝" x 6⅝", then cut diagonally in half for the corner perimeter triangles.

Borders

Note: The width of your quilt's border strips will be determined by the size of the printed pattern motifs. The widths below are the ones used in *Vintage Scrap Baskets.*

Inner Border
◆ Cut 8 strips 1¼" wide.

Middle Border
◆ Cut 4 lengthwise strips 3¼" x 84" or 8 crosswise strips 3¼" wide.

Outer Border
◆ Cut 4 lengthwise strips 7¼" x 84" or 8 crosswise strips 7¼" wide.

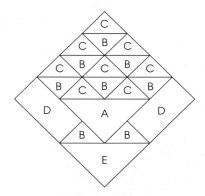

Flower Basket block

Designing the Blocks

As you cut the pieces for each block, arrange them on your design wall or board and decide if you like the combination of prints. You may want to make duplicates of any blocks you particularly like. When you are ready to sew some blocks, refer to the Flower Basket Block Sewing Guide on page 42.

Block Construction

Arrows indicate pressing direction.

1. Sew 6 B and C triangles into squares. Press toward the darker fabric and clip off the ears.

2. Attach the 2 single C triangles and sew the rows. Press the seams in opposite directions for each row.

3. Join the rows. Press in the direction of the arrows.

4. Attach the A triangle. Press.

5. Sew the 2 B triangles to the 2 D rectangles. Stitch them to the basket unit. Attach the E triangle. Press.

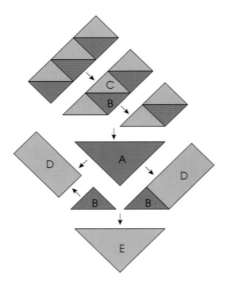

Flower Basket Block Sewing Guide

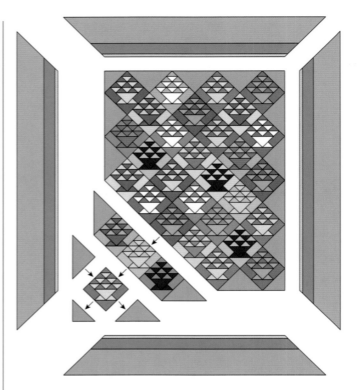

Vintage Scrap Baskets Design & Construction Guide

Quilt Top Construction

1. Arrange the blocks and perimeter triangles in the order shown on the *Vintage Scrap Baskets* Design & Construction Guide.

2. Start at the lower left-hand corner and use the One-Pin, Two-Pin Sewing Method, pages 115–117, to sew diagonal rows of basket blocks and perimeter triangles. Alternate the pressing direction of the seams from row to row. Join the rows and press all the seams in one direction.

Mitered Borders

Attaching borders with mitered corners differs from attaching straight borders. Turn to Sewing Essentials, pages 118–119, for information.

1. Measure the width and length of the quilt top. Piece, if necessary, and cut each border strip with an additional length of 24".

2. Sew 4 sets of inner, middle, and outer borders strips together. Press the seams toward the inner border.

3. Sew the borders to the quilt. Miter the corners. Press the seam toward the quilt.

Finishing

Turn to Sewing Essentials, pages 119–121, for finishing information.

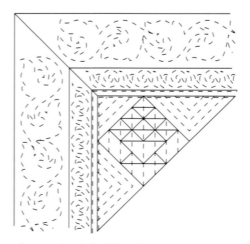

Suggested Quilting Pattern

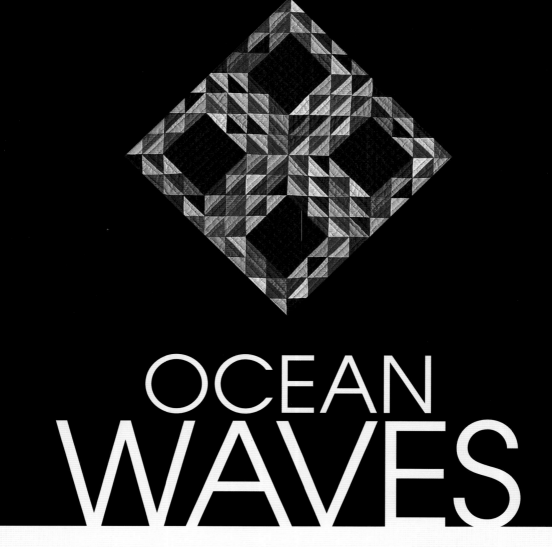

OCEAN
WAVES

’ve never met an Ocean Waves quilt I didn't like! Even the name is enticing. I love
oceans; their infinite size, the salty smell, the sound of waves pounding against the
shore. When I look at an Ocean Waves quilt, I imagine pointy little waves skipping
merrily across the surface. I'm sure whoever originated this block had a similar idea
in mind.

Anatomy of the Ocean Waves Block

The Ocean Waves block has a large center square surrounded by twenty-four
lighter-colored triangles and twenty-four darker-colored triangles. The strong value
contrast of the opposing triangles contributes to the dynamic look of the finished
quilt. The center square can be either a lighter- or a darker-colored fabric. What
makes the pattern so spectacular is that when the blocks are stitched together, they
create a powerful overall design.

MAKING WAVES

Making Waves, Frame Size: 33" x 33", Quilt Size: 34½" x 34½" (size before quilting), Gai Perry

The square size of this quilt makes it a perfect candidate for framing. If your home is decorated with a country theme, the pattern can be turned into the ultimate country quilt by choosing a collection of traditional plaids, checks, stripes, and small-scale prints.

Color and Fabric Suggestions

The use of textured and printed batiks gives the quilt a bold, contemporary look. The complementary color scheme pairs lustrous purples with rich, buttery golds. Notice how the Purple Color Family is stretched to include shades of red-violet and blue-violet. The Yellow Color Family moves from lemon to peach.

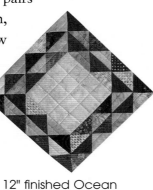

12" finished Ocean Waves block

Fabric Quantities

Work with the two Color Families mentioned above or develop your own variation of the pattern.

Blocks

Light Purple and Light Gold Batiks: ⅛ yard each of approximately 5–6 fabrics of each Color Family, approximately 1¼ yards total

Darker Purple Batiks: ⅛ yard each of approximately 10–12 fabrics, approximately 1¼ yards total

Lighter-Colored Gold Batik: ½ yard for block centers and side half-block triangles

Binding: ⅓ yard lighter- or darker-colored batik. (No binding is necessary if you are planning to frame this wallhanging.)

Backing: 1⅛ yards
Batting: 38" x 38"

Cutting

The following cutting method ensures a straight grain is stitched to a bias grain to prevent stretching.

Light Purple and Light Gold Batiks

◆ Cut 48 squares 4¼" x 4¼" (approximately 24 of each Color Family), then cut diagonally in both directions. You will need 192 triangles total.

Darker Purple Batiks

◆ Cut 96 squares 3" x 3", then cut diagonally in half. You will need 192 triangles total.

Lighter-Colored Gold Batik

◆ Cut 4 squares 6½" x 6½" for full-block centers.

◆ Cut 2 squares 9¾" x 9¾", then cut each square diagonally in both directions for half-block triangles.

Designing the Blocks

Design 4 full blocks and 8 half blocks. If you are working on a design wall, start by putting up all the pieces for the 4 full blocks, then add the 8 half blocks. Working this way will help to get an even distribution of colors and fabrics. This is important because the quilt will be hanging on the wall for all your friends to see. (Gulp, no pressure here!)

Avoid using the same fabric more than three or four times per block. Use the quilt photo and the *Making Waves* Design & Construction Guide on page 46 as your reference for placement. Try not to make any two blocks exactly alike.

When all the pieces are arranged on your design wall, squint your eyes (or use a reducing glass) to critique. Rearrange if necessary.

MAKING WAVES

Block Construction

When you are content with the placement of all the small triangles, use the following diagrams to stitch the individual blocks together.

1. Sew 4 inner pyramid triangle units. Note that 2 of the units have 3 dark triangles and 2 of the units have 3 light triangles. Press toward the darker triangles. Sew the units to the center square and press toward the pyramid triangles. Note: Pressing this direction allows the center square to lie flat and moves the seam allowances out of the way for quilting around the center square.

2. Sew 8 outer pyramid triangle units. Note that 4 units have 3 dark triangles and 4 units have 3 light triangles. Press toward the darker triangles. Sew the units together and press. Sew the combined units to the block and press.

3. To make the half blocks, sew 2 inner pyramid triangle units. Note that 1 unit has 3 dark triangles and 1 unit has 3 light triangles. Press toward the darker triangles. Sew the units to the center triangle and press toward the pyramid triangles.

4. Sew 4 outer pyramid triangle units. Note that 2 units have 3 dark triangles and 2 units have 3 light triangles. Press

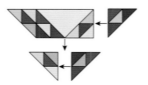

toward the darker triangles. Sew the units to the block and press.

Quilt Top Construction

1. Start at the lower left-hand corner and use the One-Pin, Two-Pin Method, pages 115–117, to sew diagonal rows of blocks together. Alternate the pressing direction of the seams from row to row.

2. Sew the rows together and press all the seams in one direction.

Making Waves Design & Construction Guide

Finishing

Turn to Sewing Essentials, pages 119–121, for finishing instructions.

Framing Information

When you finish quilting *Making Waves*, the width and length measurements might be slighter larger than the suggested 33" x 33" frame size. The quilt can be trimmed down during the framing process. Turn to page 122 for easy framing instructions.

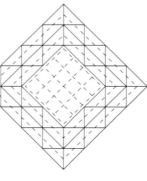

Suggested Quilting Pattern

COUNTRY WAVES

Country Waves, 71" x 83" (size before quilting), Gai Perry

COUNTRY WAVES

Setting the blocks in straight rows rather than on-point gives the Ocean Waves pattern a less formal look. This quilt could easily be enlarged to fit a twin-size bed by adding a row of blocks to the length and width and/or making wider borders.

Color and Fabric Suggestions

Scraps from dozens of traditional style plaids, checks, and tiny florals were used for the darker triangles in *Country Waves*. The lighter triangles and the block centers were made with an off-white solid. The color scheme uses the Red, Yellow, Green, and Blue Color Families.

12" finished Ocean Waves block

Fabric Quantities

Work with the Color Families and fabric styles mentioned above or develop your own variation of the pattern.

Blocks and Borders

Off-White Solid: 3¾ yards for triangles, block squares, and inner border

Darker Prints: ¼ yard each of 10–15 traditional-style prints plus additional scraps for added interest, approximately 2½ yards total, for triangles

Bright Traditional Print: 2½ yards for outer border. (You can get by with 1¼ yards if you are willing to do some piecing.)

Binding: ½ yard striped print

Backing: 4⅞ yards

Batting: 75" x 87"

Cutting

The following cutting method ensures a straight grain is stitched to a bias grain to prevent stretching.

Blocks

Cut enough fabric to design and sew 4 blocks at a time. That way the cutting process won't get too tiresome. Cut the following pattern pieces for each block. You will need 30 blocks.

Off-White Solid

Note: If cutting the inner border lengthwise, cut the border before the triangles and block centers.

◆ Cut 6 squares 4¼" x 4¼", then cut diagonally in half in both directions. (You will need 180 squares, 720 triangles total.)

◆ Cut 1 square 6½" x 6½" for the block center. (You will need 30 total.)

Darker Prints

◆ Cut 12 squares 3" x 3", then cut diagonally in half. (You will need 360 squares, 720 triangles total.)

Borders

Inner Border

◆ Cut 8 crosswise strips or 4 lengthwise strips 1¼" x 76".

Outer Border

◆ Cut 8 crosswise strips or 4 lengthwise strips 5" x 85".

Designing the Blocks

Create contrast by putting a nice mix of warm and cool colors into each block and try not to make any two blocks alike. Avoid using the same print more than three or four times per block.

Block Construction

1. Sew 4 inner pyramid triangle units. Note that 2 of the units have 3 dark triangles and 2 of the units have 3 light triangles. Press toward the darker triangles. Sew the units to the center square and press toward the pyramid triangles.

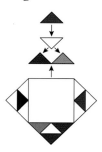

2. Sew 8 outer pyramid triangle units. Note that 4 units have 3 dark triangles and 4 units have 3 light triangles. Press toward the darker triangles. Sew the units together and press. Sew the combined units to the block and press.

Quilt Top Construction

1. Arrange the sewn blocks using the *Country Waves* Design & Construction Guide as a reference.

2. Start at the bottom and use the One-Pin, Two-Pin Sewing Method, pages 115–117, to sew the rows of blocks together. Alternate the pressing direction of the seams from row to row. Join the rows and press all the seams in one direction.

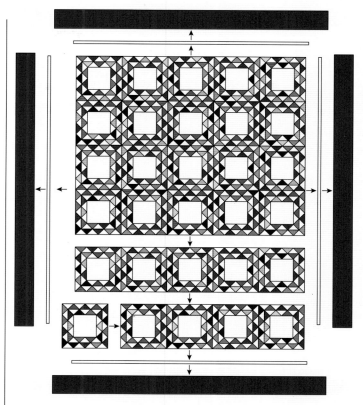

Country Waves Design & Construction Guide

Borders

1. Turn to Sewing Essentials, pages 117–118, for information on measuring and attaching borders.

2. Piece, if necessary, and trim inner border strips to the appropriate lengths. Sew them to the quilt top. Press the seams toward the border.

3. Add the outer borders in the same manner.

Finishing

Turn to Sewing Essentials, pages 119–121, for finishing instructions.

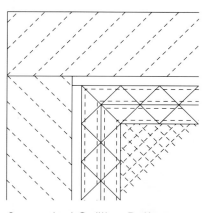

Suggested Quilting Pattern

AMISH WAVES

Amish Waves, 59½" x 59½" (size before quilting), Gai Perry

What makes this quilt design so eye-catching is the effective use of three types of contrast: first, the value contrast of dozens of lighter colors against an inky, blue-black background; second, the warm-cool contrast of warm reds, golds, and oranges with cool blues, greens, and purples; and third, the more subtle contrast of vibrant hues with duller tones.

8½" finished Ocean Waves block

Fabric Quantities

Work with solid colors or substitute prints and develop your own interpretation of the pattern.

Blocks and Borders

Lighter-Colored Solids: ⅛–¼ yard each of 12 fabrics, plus additional scraps (approximately 2 yards total) for triangles

Darker-Colored Solids: ⅛–¼ yard each of 12 fabrics (darker shades of the same colors as the lighter-colored solids), plus additional scraps (approximately 1¼ yards total) for triangles

Dark Solid: 1¼ yards for block centers, half-block triangles, inner border, and outer border

Contrasting Solid: 1⅝ yards for middle border. (You can get by with ⅜ yard if you are willing to do some piecing.)

Binding: ½ yard contrasting solid

Backing: 3⅝ yards

Batting: 63" x 63"

Cutting

Cut enough fabric to design 4 blocks at a time. If you like the way they look, sew them and then cut more triangles. Cut the following pattern pieces for each block. You will need 24 full blocks and 16 half blocks.

Lighter-Colored Solids

◆ Cut 6 squares 3⅜" x 3⅜", then cut diagonally in both directions. (You will need 192 squares, 768 triangles total.)

Darker-Colored Solids

◆ Cut 12 squares 2⅜" x 2⅜", then cut diagonally in half. (You will need 384 squares, 768 triangles total.)

Dark Solid

Note: If cutting the inner and outer borders lengthwise, cut the borders before the block centers and triangles.

◆ Cut 1 square 4¾" x 4¾" for full-block centers. (You will need 24 total.)

◆ Cut 1 square 7¼" x 7¼", then cut diagonally in half in both directions for half-block triangles You will need 4 squares, 16 triangles total.

◆ Cut 4 lengthwise strips 1½" x 53" or 6 crosswise strips 1½" wide for inner border.

◆ Cut 4 lengthwise strips 3¾" x 62" or 7 crosswise strips 3¾" wide for outer border.

Contrasting Solid

◆ Cut 4 lengthwise 1¾" x 55" strips or 6 crosswise strips 1¾" wide for middle border.

Designing The Blocks

Design and sew 24 full blocks and 16 half blocks. Put a mix of warm-cool colors and dull-bright colors into each block for contrast.

dull-bright colors into each block for contrast. Avoid using the same fabric more than three or four times per block and try not to make any two blocks exactly alike.

Block Construction

1. Sew 4 inner pyramid triangle units. Note that 2 of the units have 3 dark triangles and 2 of the units have 3 light triangles. Press toward the darker triangles. Sew the units to the center

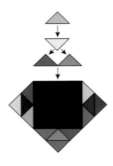

square and press toward the pyramid units.

2. Sew 8 outer pyramid triangle units. Note that 4 units have 3 dark triangles and 4 units have 3 light triangles. Press toward the darker triangles. Sew the units together and press. Sew the combined units to the block and press.

3. To make the half blocks, sew 2 inner pyramid triangle units. Note that 1 unit has 3 dark triangles and 1 unit has 3 light triangles. Press

toward the darker triangles. Sew the units to the center triangle and press toward the pyra-

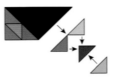

mid triangles.

4. Sew 4 outer pyramid triangle units. Note that 2 units have 3 dark triangles and 2 units have 3 light triangles. Press toward the darker

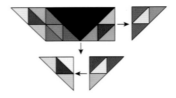

triangles. Sew the units to the block and press.

Quilt Top Construction

1. Arrange the sewn quilt blocks using the *Amish Waves* Design & Construction Guide as a reference.

2. Start at the lower left-hand corner and use the One-Pin, Two-Pin Sewing Method, pages 115–117, to sew diagonal rows of blocks together. Alternate the pressing direction of the seams from row to row. Sew the rows together and press all the seams in one direction.

Borders

1. Turn to Sewing Essentials, pages 117–118, for information on measuring and attaching borders.

2. Piece, if necessary, and trim inner border strips to the appropriate lengths. Sew them to the quilt top. Press the seams toward the border.

3. Add the middle and outer borders in the same manner.

Finishing

Turn to Sewing Essentials, pages 119–121, for finishing instructions.

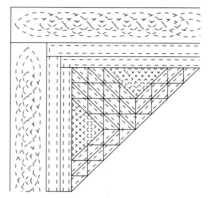

Suggested Quilting Pattern

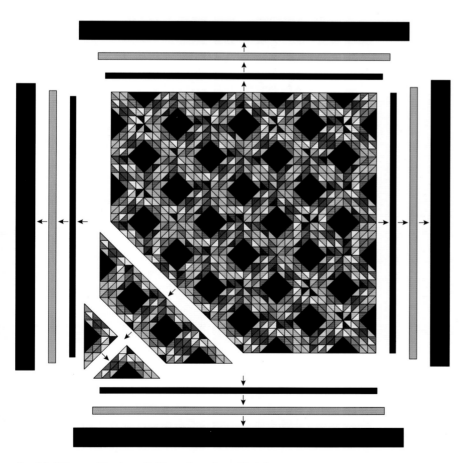

Amish Waves Design & Construction Guide

PLATES

Before I became a full-time quilter, I owned an antique shop and one of the first things I learned is that anything blue and white sells for a higher price. Blue and white quilts are the ultimate "find" and blue and white china is prized above all other color combinations. It seems as though almost every country in the world has made a special kind of blue and white china—and all of it, very collectible! Flo Blue, Delft, Spongeware, Blue Willow, Staffordshire, and Chinese export porcelain are just a few of the popular varieties.

Anatomy of the Plate Block

I designed an easy-to-sew plate block and then set the blocks in horizontal rows to give the impression of plates sitting on shelves. Each block is made with two or three fabrics; the plate rim, the center, and the background. The pattern offers endless possibilities. Wouldn't a plate collection with Christmas motifs make a beautiful holiday decoration?

BLUE PLATE
SPECIAL

Blue Plate Special, 61" x 70¾" (size before quilting), Gai Perry

BLUE PLATE SPECIAL

After I started quilting, I began to accumulate blue and white prints. I didn't know what to do with them, but I enjoyed thinking about the possibilities. Then one day I had a brainstorm! Why not make a quilt combining two of my favorite things: blue and white with china plates.

Color and Fabric Suggestions

This is what I call a one-color quilt. The white doesn't count because, technically it isn't a color. Each block has a cobalt blue and white print for the plate rim. The plate centers feature a variety of light-blue and white prints, and some of them have the same solid white fabric that was used for the background and border. The shelves were constructed with two fabrics; a light-blue and white print and a blue and white stripe.

10" finished Plate block

Fabric Quantities

Work with the blue and white color scheme mentioned above or substitute another color in combination with white.

Plates

One-Color (plus white) Prints: ¼ yard each of 7–10 fabrics for plate rims

Lighter-Colored (plus white) Prints: ¼ yard each of 4–5 fabrics plus some of the background fabric for plate centers

Background, Border, Binding, and Shelves

White Solid: 2½ yards for block background,
background, border, and binding

Lighter One-Color (plus white) Print: ⅝ yard in the same color as the plate rims, but much lighter for plate shelves (H and I)

Stripe: ⅜ yard for edge of plate shelves (J)

Backing: 3⅔ yards

Batting: 65" x 75"

Template plastic

Cutting

Blocks

Refer to the Plate Block Sewing Guide, page 57, and cut the following pieces for each block. Make a plastic template for the 10" Plate block, pattern D, on page 67. If necessary, refer to Making and Using Templates on page 115. You will need 25 blocks. It is preferable to cut and design a few blocks at a time.

One-Color (plus white) Prints

◆ Cut 4 rectangles 3" x 5½" (A). (You will need 100 rectangles total.)

◆ Cut 1 square 4¾" x 4¾", then cut diagonally in half in both directions to make 4 triangles (B). (You will need 25 squares, 100 triangles total.)

◆ Cut 2 squares 2⅛" x 2⅛", then cut diagonally in half to make 4 triangles (C). (You will need 50 squares, 100 triangles total.)

Lighter-Colored Prints

◆ Cut 1 using template (D). (You will need 25 total.)

White Solid

Note: If cutting inner and outer borders lengthwise, cut the borders before E, F, and G.

◆ Cut 2 squares 3⅝" x 3⅝", then cut diagonally in half to make 4 triangles (E). (You will need 50 squares, 100 triangles total.)

Background, Border, and Shelves

White Solid

◆ Cut 30 pieces 1¾" x 10½" (F).

◆ Cut 3 squares 3" x 3", then cut diagonally in half in both directions to make 12 triangles (G). (You will not use 2 triangles.)

◆ Cut 7 crosswise strips 2" wide. Piece, if necessary, and cut 4 strips 2" x 58" (K).

◆ Cut 3 lengthwise strips 2" x approximately 73" or cut 6 crosswise strips 2" wide for the top and side borders.

◆ Cut 1 lengthwise strip 3" x approximately 60" or cut 2 crosswise strips 3" wide for the bottom border.

Lighter One-Color Print

◆ Cut 5 squares 2⅛" x 2⅛", then cut diagonally in half to make 10 triangles (H).

◆ Cut 8 crosswise strips 1¾" wide. Piece and cut 5 strips (1¾" x 55½") (I).

Stripe

◆ Cut 8 crosswise strips 1" wide. Piece and cut 5 strips (1" x 58") (J).

Designing the Blocks

On your design wall or board, design and sew 25 blocks using the Plate Block Sewing Guide as a reference.

Note: When you study the quilt photo, you will notice that each plate rim and plate center fabric is repeated two to five times.

Block Construction

1. Sew 4 pairs of B and E triangles. Press toward the darker fabric and clip off the ears.

2. Sew Unit 1 and Unit 3. Press in the direction of the arrows.

3. Sew 4 C triangles to piece D. Sew Unit 2. Press in the direction of the arrows.

4. Join the 3 units. Press in the direction of the arrows.

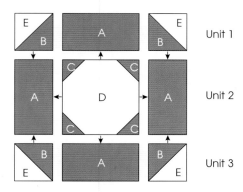

Plate Block Sewing Guide

Quilt Top Construction

1. Referring to the quilt photo on page 55 and the *Blue Plate Special* Design & Construction Guide on page 58, arrange the sewn blocks. Make sure that the duplicate blocks are evenly spaced across the surface of the quilt top.

2. Stitch the background rectangles F to the side edges of each block creating 5 rows of 5 blocks per row. Press in the direction of the arrows.

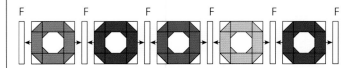

3. To make 5 shelf units, sew 10 pairs of G and H triangles into squares. Press toward the darker fabric and clip off the ears. Sew a triangle pair to each end of the I shelf. Make sure that each pair has the correct orientation. Press in the direction of the arrows.

4. Sew a J shelf to each G/H/I shelf. Press in the direction of the arrows. Attach a shelf unit to the bottom edge of each row of plates. Press.

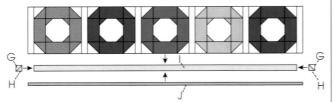

5. Sew a K background strip to the upper edge of each row of plates, with the exception of the top row. Press in the direction of the arrow. Join the 5 rows of plate blocks and press.

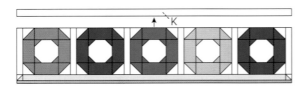

Borders

1. Refer to Sewing Essentials, pages 117–118, for information on measuring and attaching borders.

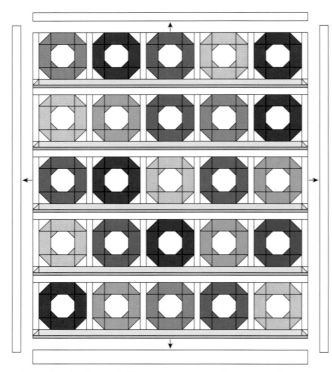

Blue Plate Special Design & Construction Guide.

2. Piece, if necessary, and trim the top and bottom borders to the appropriate lengths. Note that the top border is cut from a 2"-wide strip and bottom border is cut from a 3"-wide strip. Attach the top and bottom borders to the quilt top. Press the seams toward the border. Piece, if necessary, and cut side borders to the appropriate length. Attach the side borders to the quilt top. Press the seams toward the border.

Finishing

Turn to Sewing Essentials, pages 119–121, for finishing instructions.

Suggested Quilting

I used to have more free time. Now, I can't imagine doing this much hand quilting.

Lower right-hand corner detail

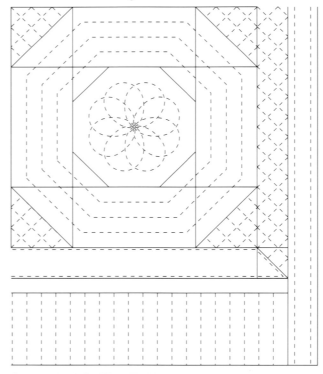

Suggested Quilting Pattern

CHINTZWARE
PLATES

Chintzware Plates, 56½" x 67¼" (size before quilting), Gai Perry

CHINTZWARE PLATES

Chintzware is a style of china tableware that was mass-produced in the early twentieth century. It has become extremely collectible in recent years. I think much of its popularity is due to the extensive articles and publicity given to it by *Victoria* magazine. In any case, the diverse and charming floral patterns that appear on this vintage china inspired *Chintzware Plates*.

Color and Fabric Suggestions

The complementary color scheme of the lavender and yellow-gold border frames a collection of multi-colored floral prints and pastel solids. Some of the fabrics look very similar to the original chintzware china patterns.

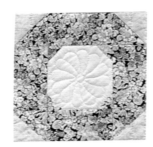
10" finished Plate block

Fabric Quantities

Work with the colors and fabric styles mentioned above or develop your own variation of the pattern.

Blocks

Floral Prints: ¼ yard each or large scraps (9½" x 12") of at least 11 fabrics for plate rims
   Note: You will be able to make 2 plates from each ¼ yard and 1 plate from each large scrap.
Solid-Colored Pastels: 16 squares 6" x 6" of at least 8 fabrics (½ yard total) for plate centers
Light-Colored Print: 1⅓ yards for background
Shelves and Borders
Contrasting Print: ⅓ yard in a color that contrasts with the background fabric for plate shelves (H and I)

Print: ¼ yard of a second print for the edge of the plate shelves (J)
Light-Colored Floral Print: 2⅛ yards for inner border. (You can get by with ¾ yard if you are willing to cut crosswise and do some piecing.)
Darker-Colored Floral Print: 2⅛ yards in a shade that will contrast with the inner border for outer border. (You can get by with ⅞ yard for the borders if you are willing to cut crosswise and do some piecing.)
Backing: 3½ yards
Binding: ½ yard
Batting: 60" x 71"

Cutting

Blocks

Refer to the Block Sewing Guide, page 61, and cut the following pieces for each block. Make a plastic template for the 10" Plate Block pattern D on page 67. If necessary, refer to Making and Using Templates on page 115. You will need 16 blocks. Cut a few of the fabrics and design 2 or 3 blocks at a time.
Floral Prints
◆ Cut 4 rectangles 3" x 5½" (A). (You will need 64 rectangles total.)
◆ Cut 1 square 4¾" x 4¾", then cut diagonally in half in both directions to make 4 triangles (B). (You will need 16 squares, 64 triangles total.)
◆ Cut 2 squares 2⅛" x 2⅛", then cut diagonally in half to make 4 triangles (C). (You will need 32 squares, 64 triangles total.)
Solid-Colored Pastels
◆ Cut 1 using template (D). (You will need 16 total.)

Light-Colored Print

- ◆ Cut 2 squares 3⅜" x 3⅜", then cut diagonally in half to make 4 triangles (E). (You will need 32 squares, 64 triangles total.)

Background, Shelves, and Borders

Light-Colored Print

- ◆ Cut 20 pieces 1½" x 10½" (F).
- ◆ Cut 2 squares 2⅝" x 2⅝", then cut diagonally in half in both directions to make 8 triangles (G).
- ◆ Cut 5–6 crosswise strips 2¼" wide. Piece, if necessary, and cut 5 strips 2¼" x 45½" (K).

Contrasting Print

- ◆ Cut 4 squares 1⅞" x 1⅞", then cut diagonally in half to make 8 triangles (H).
- ◆ Cut 4–5 crosswise strips 1½" wide. Piece, if necessary, and cut 4 strips 1½" x 43½" (I).

Print

- ◆ Cut 4–5 crosswise strips 1¼" wide. Piece, if necessary, and cut 4 strips 1¼" x 45½" (J).

Light-Colored Floral Print

- ◆ Cut 4 lengthwise strips 3" x 71" or cut 7 crosswise strips 3" wide for inner border.

Darker-Colored Floral Print

- ◆ Cut 4 lengthwise strips 3½" x 71" or cut 7 crosswise strips 3½" wide for outer border.

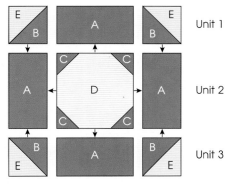

Plate Block Sewing Guide; Press in the direction of the arrows.

Designing the Blocks

Design and sew 16 blocks using the Plate Block Sewing Guide as a reference.

Design Note: Each plate rim fabric was used once or twice. Some of the plate center fabrics were used more frequently.

Block Construction

1. Sew 4 pairs of B and E triangles. Press toward the darker fabric and clip off the ears.

2. Sew Unit 1 and Unit 3. Press.

3. Sew 4 C triangles to pattern piece D. Sew Unit 2. Press.

4. Join the 3 units. Press.

Quilt Top Construction

1. Referring to the quilt photo on page 59 and the *Chintzware Plates* Design & Construction Guide on page 62 as a reference, arrange the sewn blocks. Make sure the duplicate blocks are evenly spaced across the surface of the quilt top.

2. Stitch F to the side edges of each plate block creating 4 rows of 4 blocks per row. Press in the direction of the arrows.

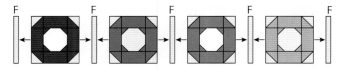

3. Sew 8 pairs of G and H triangles into squares. Press toward the darker fabric and clip off the ears. Sew a pair of triangles to each end of the I shelf. Make sure that each pair of triangles has the correct orientation. Press. Make 4.

CHINTZWARE PLATES

4. Sew a J shelf to each G/H/I unit. Press in the direction of the arrows. Attach a shelf unit to the bottom edge of each row of plates. Press.

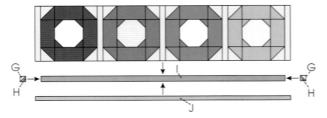
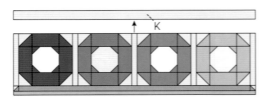

5. Sew a K background strip to the upper edge of each row of plates. Press in the direction of the arrows. Attach the fifth strip to the lower edge of the bottom shelf unit. Join the 4 rows of plates and press.

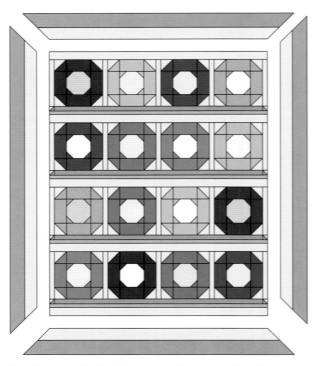

Chintzware Plates Design & Construction Guide

Borders

1. Attaching borders with mitered corners differs from attaching straight borders. Measure the width and length of the quilt top. Piece, if necessary, and cut each border strip with an additional length of 14".

2. Sew 4 sets of inner and outer border strips into pairs and press toward the inner border. See pages 118–119 to sew mitered borders.

Finishing

Turn to Sewing Essentials, pages 119–121, for finishing instructions.

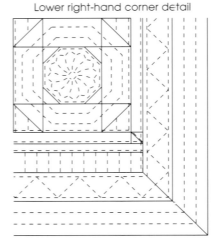

Lower right-hand corner detail

Suggested Quilting Pattern

This framed quilt is a miniature version of *Chintzware Plates.* Complete design instructions are included in my book, *Do-It-Yourself Framed Quilts.*

ORIENTAL
PLATES

Oriental Plates, 46½" x 56" (size before quilting), Gai Perry. Machine Quilted by Connie Taxiera

ORIENTAL PLATES

Here is another interpretation of the versatile 10" plate block. This quilt features an elegant assortment of oriental-style prints. The rich color scheme uses four Color Families and includes various shades of green, poppy, gold, purple, and turquoise. The background is a subtly textured print in tints of white and pale mocha.

10" finished Plate block

Fabric Quantities

Work with the colors and fabric styles mentioned above or develop your own variation of the pattern.

Blocks

Oriental-Style Prints: ⅛ yard or large scraps (9½" x 12") of 9 fabrics for plate rims

Light-Colored, Tone-on-Tone Print: 1⅛ yards for plate centers and background

Shelves, Borders, and Binding

Textured Print: ¼ yard for plate shelves (H and I)

Darker-Colored Print: ⅛ yard for edges of plate shelves (J)

Medium-Colored Print: ¼ yard print in a color that is darker than the background fabric for top and bottom scroll strips

Dark-Colored Print: 1⅓ yards for inner border. (You can get by with ⅓ yard if you are willing to cut crosswise and do some piecing.)

Oriental-Style Print: 1½ yards for outer border

and binding. (You can get by with 1 yard if you are willing to cut crosswise and do some piecing.)

Backing: 3 yards
Batting: 50" x 60"

Cutting

Blocks

Refer to the Plate Block Sewing Guide, page 65, and cut the following pieces for each block. Make a plastic template for the 10" Plate Block pattern D on page 67. If necessary, refer to Making and Using Templates on page 115. You will need 9 blocks.

Oriental-Style Prints

◆ Cut 4 rectangles 3" x 5½" (A). (You will need 36 rectangles total.)

◆ Cut 1 square 4¾" x 4¾", then cut diagonally in half in both directions to make 4 triangles (B). (You will need 9 squares, 36 triangles total.)

◆ Cut 2 squares 2⅛" x 2⅛", then cut diagonally in half to make 4 triangles (C). (You will need 18 squares, 36 triangles total.)

Light-Colored, Tone-on-Tone Print

◆ Cut 1 using template (D). (You will need 9 total.)

◆ Cut 2 squares 3⅜" x 3⅜", then cut diagonally in half to make 4 triangles (E). (You will need 18 squares, 36 triangles total.)

Background, Shelves, and Borders

Light-Colored, Tone-on-Tone Print

◆ Cut 12 pieces 1½" x 10½" (F).

◆ Cut 2 squares 2⅝" x 2⅝", then cut diagonally in half in both directions to make 8 triangles (G). (You will not use 2 triangles.)

◆ Cut 4 strips 1¾" x 34½" (K).

Textured Print

◆ Cut 3 squares 1⅞" x 1⅞", then cut diagonally in half to make 6 triangles (H).

◆ Cut 3 strips 1½" x 32½" (I).

Dark-Colored Print

◆ Cut 3 strips 1" x 34½" (J).

Medium-Colored Print

◆ Cut 2 strips 2½" x 34½" (L).

Darker-Colored Print

◆ Cut 4 lengthwise strips 1¾" x approximately 46" or cut 5 crosswise strips 1¾" wide for inner borders.

Oriental-Style Print

◆ Cut 4 lengthwise strips 5¼" x approximately 48" or cut 5–6 crosswise strips 5¼" wide for outer borders.

Designing the Blocks

Use your design wall or board to design the 9 blocks, then refer to the Plate Block Sewing Guide.

Block Construction

1. Sew 4 pairs of B and E triangles. Press toward the darker fabric and clip off the ears.

2. Sew Unit 1 and Unit 3. Press.

3. Sew 4 C triangles to pattern piece D. Sew Unit 2. Press. Join the 3 units. Press.

Quilt Top Construction

1. Referring to the quilt photo on page 63 and the *Oriental Plates* Design & Construction Guide on page 66, arrange the sewn blocks.

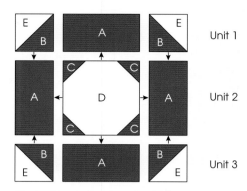

Plate Block Sewing Guide; Pressing in the direction of the arrows.

2. Stitch the background F rectangles to the side edges of each block creating 3 rows of 3 blocks per row. Press in the direction of the arrows.

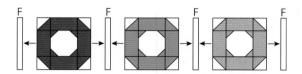

3. To make 3 plate shelf units, sew 6 pairs of G and H triangles into squares. Press toward the darker fabric and clip off the ears. Sew a triangle pair to each end of the I shelf. Make sure each pair of triangles has the correct orientation. Press in the direction of the arrows.

4. Sew a J shelf to each G/H/I unit. Press in the direction of the arrows. Attach a shelf unit to the bottom edge of each row of plates. Press.

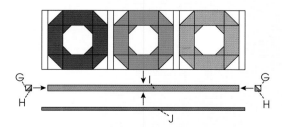

5. Sew a K background strip to the upper edge of each row of plates. Attach the fourth strip to the lower edge of the bottom row of plates. Join the 3 rows of plate blocks and press in the direction of the arrows.

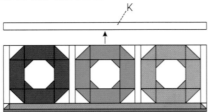

6. Attach the L scroll strips to the top and bottom edges and press toward the scroll.

Borders

1. Turn to Sewing Essentials, page 117–118, for information on measuring and attaching borders.

2. Determine the width and length of the quilt top and trim all the border strips to the appropriate lengths.

3. Attach the sides of the inner border, and then the top and bottom. Press seams toward the border.

4. Attach the outer border in the same manner.

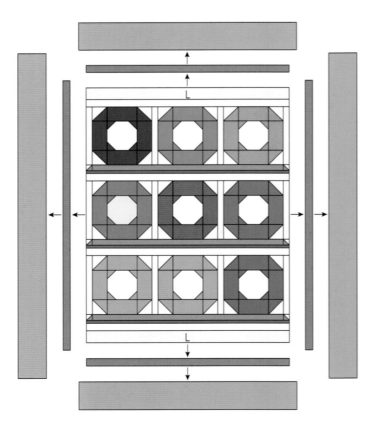

Oriental Plates Design & Construction Diagram

Lower right hand corner detail

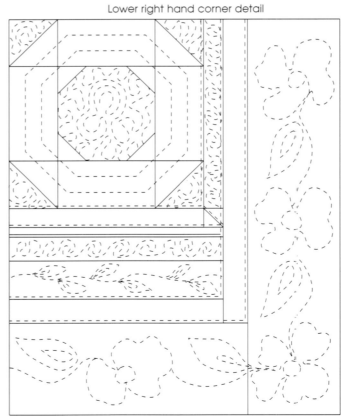

Suggested Quilting Pattern

Finishing

Turn to Sewing Essentials, pages 119–121, for finishing instructions.

Suggested Quilting

My friend Connie did a masterful job of machine quilting. The background has a meandering loop pattern and the borders are filled with lovely, free-motion leaves and flowers.

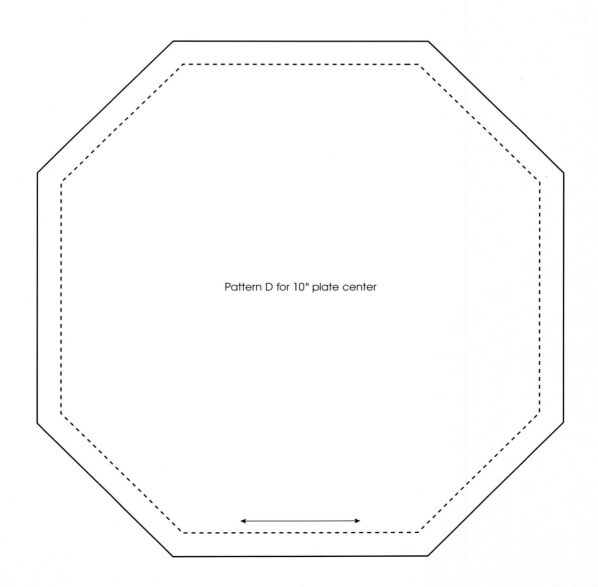

Pattern D for 10" plate center

DECO CRYSTALS

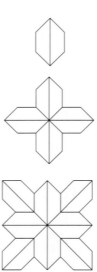

The Deco Crystals design reminds me of a decorative arts and crafts style known as *art deco* that was popular during the 1920s and 1930s. The emphasis was on simple, clean lines and bold, geometric shapes.

This original quilt pattern began its life as a doodle on graph paper. I sketched a six-sided shape that resembled a crystal. Then I drew a perpendicular line through the center and shaded the left side to establish a light and dark facet. When I added three more crystals they formed an interesting cross pattern.

I expanded the design with four more crystals set on a diagonal axis. They fit perfectly, but then of course they would because the complete crystal shape has six equal sides. I drew another round of crystals and became fascinated by the deco-style, geometric pattern that was emerging.

It dawned on me that concentric layers of crystals could be added indefinitely. What a great idea for an art quilt! But what method was I going to use to design and sew it? It looked like a nightmare of inset seams. If you're curious, read on.

MOST REQUESTED QUILT PATTERN

SHADES
OF TIFFANY

Shades of Tiffany, 51¼" x 51¼" (size before quilting), Gai Perry

I will never have the pleasure of owning a piece of stained glass by Louis Comfort Tiffany, but when I designed the Deco Crystals pattern, I thought a quilt would be the next best thing. (Well, not really, but I can pretend, can't I?)

My inspiration was a photograph of a brilliant Tiffany lampshade. When my quilt top was designed and finally sewn, I held it in front of a sunny window. To my amazement, the light shining through the quilt top turned it into a spectacular piece of stained glass. The shadows cast by the seam allowances gave the impression of leading. To preserve this illusion, I chose a light yellow fabric for the back. Now whenever I want to, I can put my quilt in front of a light source and enjoy a Tiffany-like glow.

Color and Fabric Suggestions

The rigid organization of the lighter- and darker-colored fabrics might not make *Shades of Tiffany* look like a scrap quilt but, actually, it is. There are more than 24 fabrics in the crystal area alone and the most frequently used fabrics require less than ¼ yard.

Most of the fabrics are tone-on-tone batiks, but a few additional prints were chosen for their stained glass appearance. The Yellow, Purple, Green, and Blue Color Families were used to create the predominantly cool palette.

Fabric Quantities

Work with the colors and fabric styles mentioned above and shown on the pattern quilt, or create your own variation of the color scheme.

Crystal Facets

Lighter-Colored Batiks and Prints: Scraps and ¼ yard each of 12 fabrics

Darker-Colored Batiks and Prints: Scraps and ¼ yard each of 12 fabrics

Background and Corner Posts

Light-Colored Batik: ¾ yard

Note: You may want to choose the background fabric after you have designed the crystal area of the quilt.

Leading, Borders, and Binding

Black Solid: 1 yard for leading, inner border, and binding

Darker-Colored Batiks: ⅓ yard each of 2 fabrics for middle border

Lighter-Colored Batik: ½ yard for outer border of a lighter shade of the color used for the middle border

Backing: 3 yards

Batting: 54" x 54"

Cutting

It is imperative that you make an accurate template! Trace the Shades of Tiffany facet pattern on page 75.

Crystal Facets

Lighter-Colored Batiks and Prints
◆ Cut at least 8 crystal facets from each of the selected fabrics. (Cut more as needed.)

Darker-Colored Batiks and Prints
◆ Cut at least 8 crystal facets from each of the selected fabrics. (Cut more as needed.)

Background and Corner Posts

Lighter-Colored Batik
◆ Cut 40 squares 2¼" x 2¼", then cut diagonally in half for 80 small triangles of background for the fifth round.
◆ Cut 2 squares 8⅞" x 8⅞" from the background fabric, then cut diagonally in half

for the large background corner triangles.

◆ Cut 4 squares 3" x 3" (D).

Leading and Borders

Note: You may need to adjust the sizes listed below depending on the measurements of the center of your quilt. Sew the quilt center and measure it *before* you cut the borders. Adjust the lengths of the strips as needed.

Black Solid

◆ Cut 7 crosswise strips 1" wide. Piece as necessary and cut strips into 12 strips 1" x 3" (A), 2 strips 1" x 45¾" (H), 2 strips 1" x 50¼" (J), and 12 strips 1" x 2¼" (G).

◆ Cut 2 crosswise strips 2" x 37¾" and 2 crosswise strips 2" x 40¾" for inner border.

Darker-Colored Batiks

◆ Cut 4 strips 3" x 19⅞" from each of the 2 darker-colored batiks (B) and (C) for a total of 8 strips.

Lighter-Colored Batik

◆ Cut 5 crosswise strips 2¼" wide, then cut into 8 strips 2¼" x 12⅜" (F), 4 strips 2¼" x 21" (E), and 4 squares 2¼" x 2¼" (I).

Designing the Crystal Area

Each crystal unit is composed of a lighter- and darker-colored facet. The completed crystal area contains 8 mirror-imaged sections. In the following design steps, a two-faceted crystal is referred to as a unit.

The design must be completed on your design wall before it can be sewn. If you don't have a design wall, make an accurate paste-up or use the smaller crystal pattern on page 78. Helpful Hints:

1. Put a bold color combination in the center cross.

2. Every once in a while, add some very light-colored crystal facets for sparkle.

3. As you work toward the perimeter, create a color balance with a few warm and cool fabric combinations.

4. As the design develops and you have a better understanding of the pattern, you will probably do a lot of shifting and rearranging of the crystal facets.

Crystal Area Preparation

1. Begin the design by putting the 4 crystal units selected for the center cross on your design wall. Then add the 4 diagonal crystal units. This is the first round.

2. Add the second round of crystal units.

3. Add the third round of crystal units.

4. Add the fourth round of crystal units

5. Add the fifth round of crystal units and the 80 small triangles of background fabric.

6. Move away from your design wall and decide if the crystal area is as good as you can make it. Does it project a feeling of stained glass? Don't start sewing until you are thrilled with the design. Why? Because the sewing requires total concentration and when you're finally finished, you want to have a quilt top that leaves you breathless.

Quilt Top Construction

For sewing purposes, the crystal area is divided into 8 mirror-imaged sections. Each section is labeled Section 1 or Section 2. You will have to sew 4 Section 1 units and 4 Section 2 units. (The large background corner triangles will be added later.)

The sewing method is somewhat similar to stitching a log cabin block. Crystal facets will be sewn into strips and then the strips will be joined in a back and forth, alternating pattern. Begin by sewing Section 1 (at top of the crystal area) and work in a clockwise direction.

Section 1 Sewing Guide

Arrows on the illustrations indicate the pressing direction.

1. Sew strips 1 and 2. Press. Join strips 1 and 2 and press.

2. Sew strip 3. Press. Join it to the previously constructed strip unit and press.

3. Sew strip 4 and press. Join it to the previously constructed strip unit and press.

4. Sew strip 5 and press. Join it to the previously constructed strip unit and press.

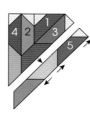

5. Sew 6 and press. Join it to the previously constructed strip unit and press.

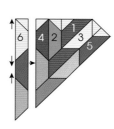

6. Sew strip 7 and press. Join it to the previously constructed strip unit and press.

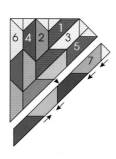

7. Sew strip 8 and press. Join it to the previously constructed strip unit and press.

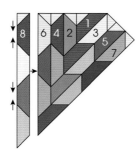

8. Sew strip 9 and press. Join it to the previously constructed strip unit and press.

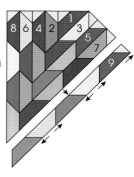

9. Sew strip 10 and press. Join it to the previously constructed strip unit and press.

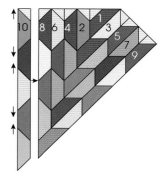

Section 2 Sewing Guide

1. Sew strips 1 and 2. Press. Join strips 1 and 2 and press.

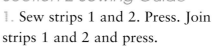

2. Sew strip 3. Press. Join it to the previously constructed strip unit and press.

3. Sew strip 4 and press. Join it to the previously constructed strip unit and press.

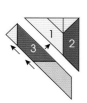

4. Sew strip 5 and press. Join it to the previously constructed strip unit and press.

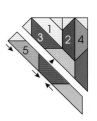

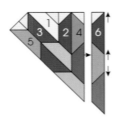

5. Sew 6 and press. Join it to the previously constructed strip unit and press.

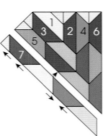

6. Sew strip 7 and press. Join it to the previously constructed strip unit and press.

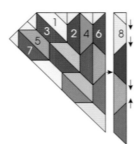

7. Sew strip 8 and press. Join it to the previously constructed strip unit and press.

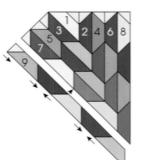

8. Sew strip 9 and press. Join it to the previously constructed strip unit and press.

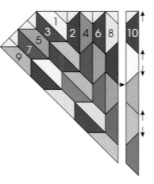

9. Sew strip 10 and press. Join it to the previously constructed strip unit and press.

Sewing the Crystal Sections Together

1. Working clockwise, join each Section 1 to a Section 2 and press the seam open. There will now be 4 sections instead of 8.

2. Join the 2 sections on the right side of the crystal area and press the seam open.

3. Join the 2 sections on the left side of the crystal area and press the seam open.

4. Sew the resulting 2 sections together and press the seam open.

5. Now sew a large background corner triangle to each corner of the crystal area and press toward the triangles.

Borders

Because of the many seams in the crystal area, the finished size will differ from quilter to quilter. The variance will depend on how the template is cut and the interpretation of the ¼" seam allowances. Translated, this means everyone cuts and sews differently. Whether the cutting measurements given for the border fabrics will be accurate for your quilt is questionable. The bottom line is that you will have to measure the completed crystal area and adjust the border lengths as needed. Turn to Sewing Essentials, pages 117–118, for measuring and attaching borders.

1. Sew the inner border strips to the upper and lower edge of the quilt top. Press the seams toward the border.

2. Sew the inner border strips to the sides of the quilt top. Press seams toward the border.

3. Sew the middle border strips B and C to leading strips A and corners D as shown. Press in the direction of the arrows. Make 2 top and bottom borders and 2 side borders.

4. Noting the orientation of the B and C strips on the photo, sew the 2 top and bottom border sections to the upper and lower edges of the quilt top and press toward the inner border.

Top and Bottom Middle Borders—Make 2.

5. Noting the orientation of the B and C strips, sew the 2 side sections to the sides of the quilt top and press toward the inner border.

Side Middle Border—Make 2.

6. Sew the outer border strips E and F to the leading strips G, corners I, and leading strips H and J as shown. Press in the direction of the arrows.

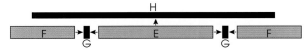

Top and Bottom Outer Border—Make 2.

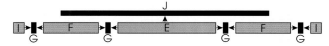

Side Outer Border—Make 2.

Yeah! The quilt top is finished!

Finishing

Turn to Sewing Essentials, pages 119–121, for finishing instructions.

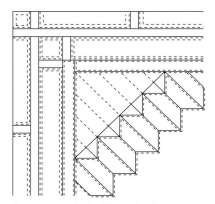

Suggested Quilting Pattern

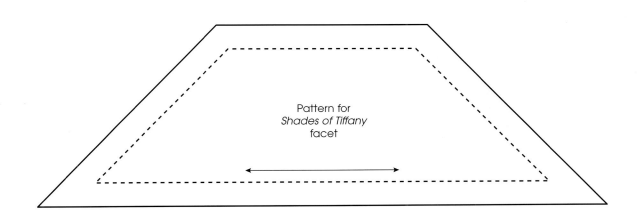

Pattern for
Shades of Tiffany
facet

DECO
MEDALLION

Deco Medallion, Frame size: 20" x 20", Quilt size: 18½" x 18½" (size before quilting), Gai Perry

Deco Medallion is made with a smaller template and has fewer crystal repeats than the previous quilt. Even so, the color combination has a stunning impact against the wide, double mat and narrow, black frame.

Color and Fabric Suggestions

The palette is a striking mixture of yellow-gold and red-violet batiks paired with a soft, blush-and-cream textured print. I've also used my favorite pansy fabric and a gold-overlay, contemporary print. The stark black background adds to the drama.

Fabric Quantities

Use the colors mentioned above and shown on the pattern quilt, or design your own variation of the color scheme.

Crystal Facets
Lighter-Colored Fabrics: Scraps of 4 fabrics
Darker-Colored Fabrics: Scraps of 3 fabrics
Background, Border, and Optional Binding
Black or Dark-Colored Solid: ⅝ yard
Backing: ⅔ yard
Batting: 22" x 22"

Cutting

An accurate template is very important! Trace the Deco Medallion facet pattern on page 79 and cut the necessary number of lighter- and darker-colored facets. You will probably end up cutting more than you need as you play with the arrangement, but that's okay, save them for another quilt.

Crystal Facets

Lighter-Colored Fabrics
◆ Cut at least 4 crystal facets from each of the selected fabrics. (Cut more as needed.)
Darker-Colored Fabrics
◆ Cut at least 4 crystal facets from each of the selected fabrics. (Cut more as needed.)

Background and Border

Black or Dark-Colored Solid
◆ Cut 20 squares 1¾" x 1¾", then cut diagonally in half to make 40 triangles for background.
◆ Cut 2 squares 3⅜" x 3⅜", then cut diagonally in half to make 4 corner triangles for background.
◆ Cut 2 crosswise strips 3" wide for borders.

Crystal Area Preparation

Each crystal unit is composed of a lighter- and darker-colored facet. The completed crystal area contains 8 mirror-imaged sections. If you compare this to *Shades of Tiffany*, you will notice that the center crystals have been rotated a quarter turn on this pattern. In the following design steps, a two-faceted crystal is referred to as a unit. The design must be completed on your design wall or board before it can be sewn.

1. Start the design by putting the lighter and darker crystal facets selected for the center X on your design surface. Now add the north, south, east, and west crystal units. This step is the first round.

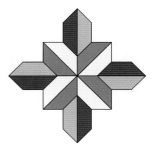

DECO MEDALLION

2. Add a second round of crystal units.

3. Add a third round of crystal units to the diagonal sections only. Then add the background triangles to create the perimeter edges.

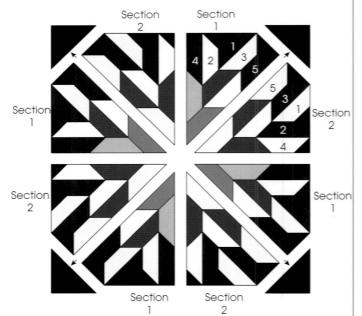

Quilt Top Construction

For sewing purposes, the crystal area is divided into 8 mirror-imaged sections. Each section is labeled Section 1 or Section 2. You will have to sew 4 Section 1 units and 4 Section 2 units. (The large background triangles shown

on the above diagram will be added later.)

The sewing method is somewhat similar to stitching a Log Cabin block. Crystal facets will be sewn into strips and then the strips will be joined in a back and forth, alternating pattern. Begin by sewing Section 1 (at top of the crystal area) and then work in a clockwise direction.

Section 1 Sewing Guide
Press the direction the arrows indicate.

Step One: Sew strips 1 and 2. Press. Join strips 1 and 2 and press.

Step Two: Sew strip 3. Press. Join it to the previously constructed strips and press.

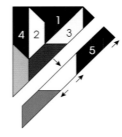

Step Three: Sew Strip 4. Press. Join it to the previously constructed strips and press.

Step Four: Sew Strip 5. Press. Join it to the previously constructed strips and press.

Section 2 Sewing Guide
Sewing the Crystal Sections Together

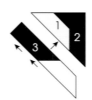
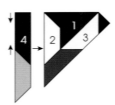

Step One: Sew strips 1 and 2. Press. Join strips 1 and 2 and press.

Step Two: Sew strip 3. Press. Join it to the previously constructed strips and press.

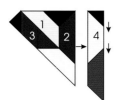

Step Three: Sew Strip 4. Press. Join it to the previously constructed strips and press.

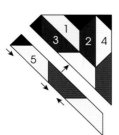

Step Four: Sew Strip 5. Press. Join it to the previously constructed strips and press.

1. Working clockwise, join each Section 1 to a Section 2 and press the seam open. There will now be 4 sections instead of 8.

2. Join the 2 sections on the right side of the crystal area and press the seam open.

3. Join the 2 sections on the left side of the crystal area and press the seam open.

4. Sew the resulting 2 sections together and press the seam open.

5. Now, sew a large background corner triangle to each corner of the crystal area and press toward the triangles.

Borders

1. Turn to Sewing Essentials, pages 117–118, for information on measuring and attaching borders.

2. Determine the width and length of the quilt top and cut all the border strips to the appropriate lengths.

3. Attach the top and bottom borders, then the side borders and press seams toward the border strips.

Note: The border strips allow mat size flexibility during the framing process.

Finishing

Turn to Sewing Essentials, pages 119–121, for finishing instructions.

Framing Information

When you are finished quilting *Deco Medallion*, do not bind it. Trim the backing fabric and the batting to 1" beyond the edge of the quilt top. Heavy quilting will shrink the size of the quilt so it will fit perfectly within the precut mat opening. Turn to page 122 for easy, do-it-yourself framing instructions.

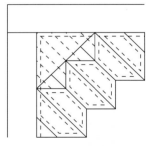

Suggested Quilting Pattern

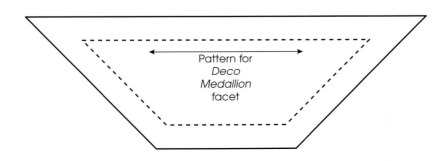

Pattern for *Deco Medallion* facet

CORN
AND BEANS

On a Spring day in 1985, I was strolling through the yard goods section of a local department store when I spotted a fabulous collection of men's shirting materials. There must have been a dozen large-scale plaids mixed in with several "manly-style" weaves and button-down stripes. Best of all, they were on sale! I'd never seen these kinds of fabrics in quilt stores before. Back then, mini-checks, homespuns, and tiny florals were the popular flavors.

Well, naturally I had to buy some, but which ones? I couldn't make up my mind, so I did what any red-blooded quilter would have done . . . I bought a half yard of everything!

Anatomy of the Corn and Beans Block

The block contains twelve pattern pieces: two large triangles and ten smaller ones. Usually, it is made with two value-contrasting fabrics, but if you look closely at the pattern quilt, you will see that some of the blocks have an additional fabric or two.

COUNTRY
COUSINS

Country Cousins, 53" x 63½" (size before quilting), Gai Perry

This is the first quilt I made with the men's shirting fabrics. It turned out to be a real "comfort quilt" and I think its popularity is due to the friendly color scheme. It's the kind of quilt you want to curl up under and watch a favorite TV show, or take a nap. Although the pattern is named Corn and Beans, according to Jinny Beyer in her book, *The Quilter's Album of Blocks and Borders*, it is also referred to as Ducks and Ducklings, Handy Andy, Hens and Chicks, and Shoo-fly.

Color and Fabric Suggestions

Country Cousins was made with an assortment of plaids, stripes, textured weaves—plus one paisley print for a slight touch of whimsy. It also has one solid color fabric. It's interesting to notice how some of the larger-scale plaids create an illusion of transparency. (Unplanned, but nice.) The color

7½" finished Corn and Beans block

scheme combines mellow shades of gold, taffy, and cinnamon from the Yellow Color Family and a range of powder blues, blue-grays, and navys from the Blue Color Family.

Fabric Quantities

Work with the colors and fabric styles mentioned above and shown on the pattern quilt, or develop your own variation of the color scheme.

Lighter-Colored Prints: ⅜ yard each of at least 10 fabrics (plus additional scraps)

Darker-Colored Prints: ⅜ yard each of at least 10 fabrics (plus additional scraps)

Binding: ½ yard of a dark solid

Backing: 3¼ yards

Batting: 57" x 67"

Cutting

Refer to the Block Sewing Guide, page 83, and cut the following pieces for each block. You will need 50 blocks.

Note: The following cutting method ensures a straight grain is stitched to a bias grain to prevent stretching. However, if you want the grain of all the plaids in a block to go in the same direction, cut the light B triangles in the same way that you cut the dark D triangles. You will need to be careful when sewing and pressing to prevent stretching.

Blocks

Lighter-Colored Prints

◆ Cut 1 square 5⅞" x 5⅞", then cut diagonally in half to make 2 triangles (A). (Save 1 triangle for another block. You will need 25 squares, 50 triangles total.)

◆ Cut 2 squares 4¼" x 4¼", then cut diagonally in half in both directions to make 8 triangles (B). (Save 3 triangles for another block. You will need 63 squares, 250 triangles total.)

Darker-Colored Prints

◆ Cut 1 square 5⅞" x 5⅞", then cut diagonally in half to make 2 triangles (C). (Save 1 triangle for another block. You will need 25 squares, 50 triangles total.)

◆ Cut 3 squares 3⅜" x 3⅜", then cut diagonally in half to make 6 triangles (D). (Save 1 tri angle for another block. You will need 125 squares, 250 triangles total.)

Lighter- and Darker-Colored Prints

Note: (You may choose to have an even scrappier look by cutting more squares to make the perimeter triangles.)

◆ Cut 5 squares 12" x 12", then cut diagonally in half in both directions to make 20 perimeter triangles. (You will not use 2 triangles.)

◆ Cut 2 squares 6¼" x 6¼", then cut diagonally in half to make 4 corner triangles.

Designing the Blocks

Make 50 blocks. When a scrap quilt involves nothing more than a repeat of the same block, its success depends on an attractive variety (and the artistic placement) of fabrics. With this in mind, it's a good idea to cut, design, and sew as you go. That way, you will have control of the developing quilt. If you like the way a particular block looks, repeat it two or three more times. Place the sewn squares on your design wall or board and critique.

As you are designing the individual blocks, mix warm with cool colors, plaids with stripes, and even dare to cut a print off-grain once in awhile. Use the Corn and Beans Block Sewing Guide as a reference. Note: Arrows on diagrams indicate pressing direction.

Block Construction

1. Sew 3 pairs of B and D triangles together. Press the seams toward the darker fabric and clip off the ears.

2. Add the single B and D triangles. Press the seams in the direction of the arrows and clip off the ears.

3. Sew the 3 rows together. Press the seams in one direction.

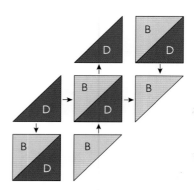

Corn and Beans Block
Sewing Guide

4. Attach the 2 large A and C triangles. Press the seams toward A and C and clip off the ears.

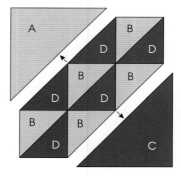

Quilt Top Construction

1. Arrange the sewn blocks and perimeter triangles using the *Country Cousins* Design & Construction Guide on page 84 as a reference.

2. Start at the lower left hand corner and use the One-Pin, Two-Pin Sewing Method, pages 115–117, to sew diagonal rows of blocks and perimeter triangles. Alternate the pressing direction of the seams from row to row.

3. Join the rows and press all the seams in one direction only.

Finishing

Turn to Sewing Essentials, pages 119–121, for finishing instructions.

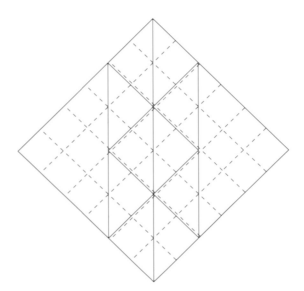

Suggested Quilting Pattern

Country Cousins Design & Construction Guide

ANALOGOUS
WEAVE

Analogous Weave, Frame Size: 35" x 35", Quilt Size: 36½" x 36½" (size before quilting), Gai Perry

I love to paint and over the years I've worked with water colors, oils, and acrylics. When I started quilting, it was natural to think of fabric as just another painting medium. Recently I've been framing some of my smaller quilts and the only surprise is that I didn't start doing it sooner.

The framed *Analogous Weave* is the perfect size quilt to hang over a mantle. Add a couple of pots of trailing ivy and a pair of candlesticks and you'll have an impressive addition to your living room decor.

The analogous (adjoining) Color Families of Blue and Purple were used to create this abstract design. The blues move all the way to turquoise and a few of the purples nudge red-violet. Several sparkling light blue and white prints and a few touches of lemon yellow were added as focal points. Most of the print styles can be categorized as contemporary.

6" finished Corn and Beans block

Fabric Quantities

Work with the colors and fabric styles mentioned above and shown on the project quilt or develop your own variation of the color scheme.

Lighter-Colored Prints: ¼ yard each of at least 12 fabrics

Darker-Colored Prints: ¼ yard each of at least 12 fabrics

Binding: ⅓ yard of a darker solid. (No binding is necessary if you are planning to frame this wall hanging.)

Backing: 1¼ yards

Batting: 40" x 40"

Cutting

The following cutting method ensures a straight grain is stitched to a bias grain to prevent stretching. Refer to the Block Sewing Guide, page 87, and cut the following pieces for each block. You will need 36 blocks.

Blocks

Lighter-Colored Prints

◆ Cut 1 square 4⅞" x 4⅞", then cut diagonally in half to make 2 triangles (A). (Save 1 triangle for another block. You will need 18 squares, 36 triangles total.)

◆ Cut 2 squares 4¼" x 4¼", then cut diagonally in half in both directions to make 8 triangles (B). (Save 3 triangles for another block. You will need 45 squares, 180 triangles total.)

Darker-Colored Prints

◆ Cut 1 square 4⅞" x 4⅞", then cut diagonally in half to make 2 triangles (C). (Save 1 triangle for another block. You will need 18 squares, 36 triangles total.)

◆ Cut 3 squares 2⅞" x 2⅞", then cut diagonally in half to make 6 triangles (D). (Save 1 triangle for another block. You will need 90 squares, 180 triangles total.)

Designing the Blocks

Because the quilt will be framed, every block is visually important. If you have a design wall, it would be wise to put up all the pieces before you start sewing. That way you can be assured of an equal distribution of color and fabric pattern. If you are working on a design board, you will have to design and sew a few blocks at a time.

Look at the project quilt and notice how the yellow print forms an irregular triangle. Why did I arrange it this way? Because I've learned that using the lightest, darkest, or brightest fabric to create a visual triangle is an artful way to lead the viewer's eye around the surface of the quilt.

Once all the pieces are in place, start sewing the individual blocks. Use the Corn and Beans Block Sewing Guide as a reference. Note: Arrows on diagrams indicate pressing direction.

Block Construction

1. Sew 3 pairs of B and D triangles together. Press the seams toward the darker fabric and clip off the ears.

2. Add the single B and D triangles. Press the seams in the direction of the arrows and clip off the ears.

3. Sew the 3 rows together. Press the seams in one direction.

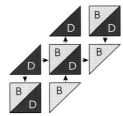

4. Attach the 2 large A and C triangles. Press the seams toward A and C and clip off the ears.

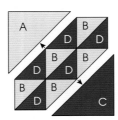

Corn and Beans
Block Sewing Guide

Quilt Top Construction

1. Use the *Analogous Weave* Design & Construction Guide as a reference to arrange the sewn blocks.

2. Start at the bottom and use the One-Pin, Two-Pin Sewing Method, pages 115–116, to sew the individual rows of blocks together. Alternate the pressing direction of the seams from row to row.

3. Join the rows and press all the seams in one direction.

Analogous Weave Design & Construction Guide

Finishing

Turn to Sewing Essentials, pages 119–121, for finishing instructions.

Framing Information

When you finish quilting *Analogous Weave*, do not bind it. At this point, the width and length measurements might be slightly larger than the suggested 35" x 35" frame size. The quilt can be trimmed down during the framing process. Turn to page 122 for easy, do-it-yourself framing instructions.

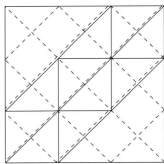

Suggested Quilting Pattern

Quilts made with representational blocks like houses and trees are always popular because they focus on a recognizable object. I have a wonderful little book entitled, *Patchwork Pictures*, by Carol LaBranche. It gives an extensive variety of patterns for flowers, baskets, trees, houses, animals, and alphabets. If you can find a copy, it will definitely be an asset to your quilting book library.

Anatomy of the Tree Block

My tree design differs from the classic Tree of Paradise block in that it has a longer, narrower trunk and four tiers of leaves instead of three. The extra row makes the tree look more imposing and provides the opportunity to use lots of scraps. Each tree block has 40 lighter and 48 darker triangles in the leaf area. When you study the quilt photograph, you will notice that the color placement of the darker leaf triangles is consistent from block to block (with the exception of the first and last vertical rows), but the color placement of the lighter leaf triangles is random and keeps changing.

ALIEN FOREST

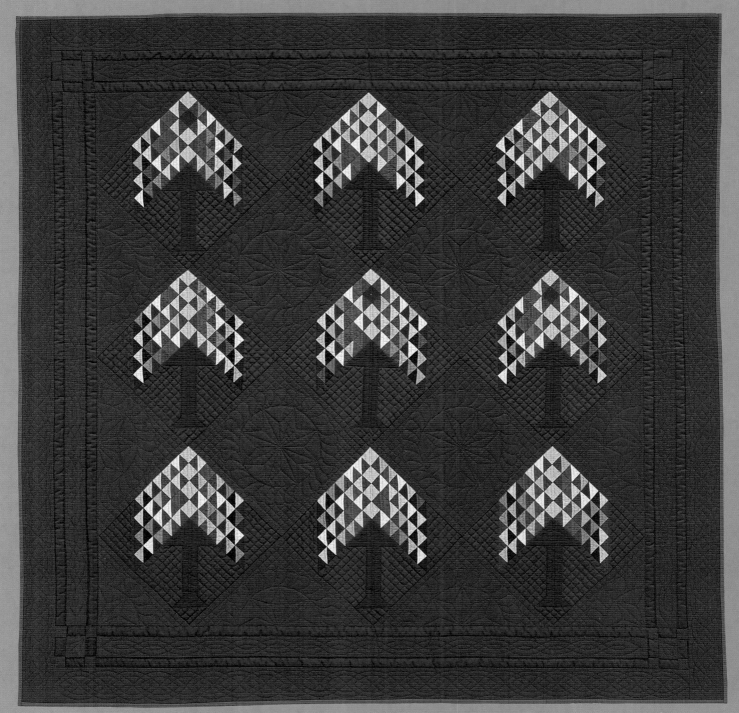

Alien Forest, 66½" x 66½" (size before quilting), Gai Perry

ALIEN FOREST

I made *Alien Forest* several years ago and I remember spending hours drawing different kinds of trees in an effort to come up with an original design. The graph paper gradually began to resemble a forest and inspired the quilt's name.

A science fiction book I was reading gave me an idea for the color scheme. I envisioned a landscape where trees were made of frozen crystal and their delicate leaves sparkled under a pale, alien sun. (Oh, yes, I have a rich fantasy life.)

Color and Fabric Suggestions

Alien Forest was made with solid-color fabrics. If you don't have a plentiful supply or a nearby source, the same effect can be achieved with printed textures and batiks.

The lighter-colored leaf triangles were made with 3 different tints of turquoise, 2 pinks, 2 peaches, 2 greens, 2 lavenders, and 1 hot pink. The darker-colored leaf triangles were made with shades of royal blue, emerald green, amethyst, dark-bright red, olive, maroon, and navy blue. The tree trunks were also made with navy blue. Contrasting shades of red-violet and a dark green were used for the background and borders.

12½" finished *Alien Forest* block (Tree of Paradise Variation)

The sparkle effect was achieved by making some of the lighter triangles almost as dark as the darker triangles and combining clear and gray-toned colors for contrast. Turquoise also adds to the illusion because, for a reason unknown to me, it's a catalyst color. It makes all the surrounding colors look brighter.

Fabric Quantities

Work with the colors and fabrics mentioned above or create your own variation of the color scheme.

Blocks
Lighter-Colored Solids: ⅛ yard each (or 9" x 14" or 11" x 12" scraps) of 12–15 fabrics for leaves and small squares
Darker-Colored Solids: ¼ yard each (or 12" x 12" or 9" x 16" scraps) of 7 fabrics
Dark-Colored Solid: ½ yard dark fabric for tree trunks
Block Background, Alternate Squares, and Borders
Cool-Colored, Dark Solid: 1¾ yards for block background and inner border
Contrasting, Warm-Colored Solid: 2⅝ yards for alternate squares and inner and outer borders
Binding: ½ yard warm-colored solid
Backing: 4 yards
Batting: 70" x 70"
Template plastic

Cutting

Refer to the Block Sewing Guide, page 91, and cut the following pieces for each block. The following cutting method ensures a straight grain is stitched to a bias grain to prevent stretching. You will need 9 blocks. Make a plastic template from Alien Forest Pattern H on page 93. If necessary, refer to Making and Using Templates on page 115.
Lighter-Colored Solids
◆ Cut 4 lighter-colored squares 1¾" x 1¾" (A). (You will need 36 squares total.)
◆ Cut 10 lighter-colored squares 3" x 3", then cut diagonally in half in both directions to make 40 triangles (B). (You will need 90

squares, 360 triangles total.)

Darker-Colored Solids

- Cut 24 darker-colored squares 2⅛" x 2⅛", then cut diagonally in half to make 48 triangles (C). (You will need 216 squares, 432 triangles total.)

Dark-Colored Solid

- Cut 1 square 4⅝" x 4⅝", then cut diagonally in half to make 1 tree trunk triangle (E). (Use the extra triangle for the next block. You will need 5 squares, 10 triangles total. You will not use 1 triangle.)

- Cut 1 rectangle 2" x 6⅝" to make 1 tree trunk (F). (You will need 9 rectangles total.)

- Cut 1 square 1⅞" x 1⅞", then cut diagonally in half to make 2 tree trunk base triangles (G). (You will need 9 squares, 18 triangles total.)

Cool-Colored, Dark Solid: for block background and inner border

- Cut 1 square 5⅞" x 5⅞", then cut diagonally in half to make 2 large background triangles (D). (You will need 9 squares, 18 triangles total.)

- Cut 2 pieces using template (H and H reversed). (You will need 9 and 9 reversed.)

- Cut 1 square 3⅜" x 3⅜", then cut diagonally in half to make 1 triangle (I). Use the extra triangle for the next block. (You will need 5 squares, 10 triangles total. You will not use 1 triangle.)

- Cut 8 lengthwise strips 1½" x approximately 56" or cut 12 crosswise strips 1½" wide for inner border fabric.

- Cut 16 rectangles 1½" x 2¼" for Nine-Patch inner border corner blocks.

Contrasting, Warm-Colored Solid: for alternate squares and middle and outer borders

- Cut 4 squares 13" x 13" for alternate squares.

- Cut 2 squares 19" x 19", then cut diagonally in half, in both directions, to make 8 perimeter triangles.

- Cut 2 squares 9¾" x 9¾", then cut diagonally in half to make 4 corner triangles.

- Cut 4 lengthwise strips 2¼" x approximately 56" or cut 6 crosswise strips 2¼" wide for middle border.

- Cut 16 squares 1½" x 1½" and 4 squares 2¼" x 2¼" for Nine-Patch middle border corner blocks.

- Cut 4 lengthwise strips 3½" x 69" or cut 8 crosswise strips 3½" wide for outer border.

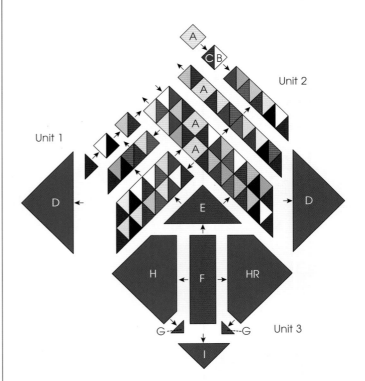

Alien Forest Block Sewing Guide

Designing the Blocks

Arrange the pieces for the first block on your design wall or board and critique. Decide if there is an exciting variety of the lighter-colored triangles. Does the leaf area sparkle? When you are satisfied with the block, sew it using the *Alien Forest* Block Sewing Guide, page 91, as a reference.

Block Construction

1. Sew 40 B and C triangles into squares to make the leaves in Units 1 and 2. Press toward the darker fabric and clip off the ears. Join the A squares and B/C squares into rows. Sew a single C triangle to the end of each row of leaves. Press in the direction of the arrows. Sew the rows of squares together. Press in the direction of the arrows.

2. To make Unit 3, sew 2 G triangles to 2 H pattern pieces. Press in the direction of the arrows. Sew a G/H Unit to either side of the F rectangle. Attach the E and I triangles.

3. Sew Unit 1 to Unit 3. Press. Attach Unit 2 and press.

4. Design and sew 8 more blocks and try not to make any two exactly alike.

Quilt Top Construction

1. Arrange the tree blocks, the alternate blocks, and the perimeter triangles in the order shown on the *Alien Forest* Design & Construction Guide.

2. Start at the lower left-hand corner and use the One-Pin, Two-Pin Sewing Method, pages 115–117, to sew diagonal rows together. Press toward alternate blocks and perimeter triangles.

3. Join the rows and press all the seams in one direction.

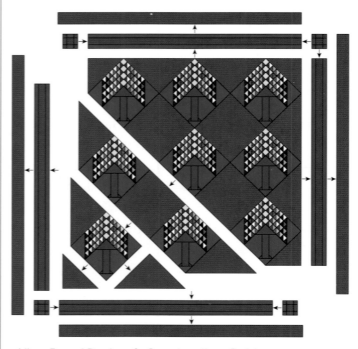

Alien Forest Design & Construction Guide

Borders

1. Turn to Sewing Essentials, pages 117–118, for information on measuring and attaching borders.

2. Measure the width and length of the quilt top and trim all the border strips to the appropriate lengths.

3. Stitch a 1½"-wide border strip to each side of a 2¼"-wide border strip and press toward the narrow strips.

4. Attach a border unit to the right and left side of the quilt top. Press toward the border.

5. Make 4 Nine-Patch inner border corner blocks. Press in the direction of the arrows.

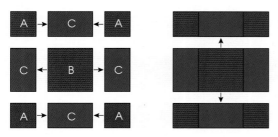

Nine-Patch Assembly Guide

6. Sew a Nine-Patch block to each end of the 2 remaining border units. Attach these units to the top and bottom of the quilt.

7. Attach outer borders to the quilt top. Press toward the outer border.

Finishing

Turn to Sewing Essentials, pages 119–121, for finishing instructions.

Suggested Quilting

The quilting pattern for the tree blocks is shown here. I used a precut stencil with a feathered wreath and star for the alternate blocks and perimeter triangles. Two different size precut cable stencils were used for the borders. Refer to the *Alien Forest* photograph for ideas.

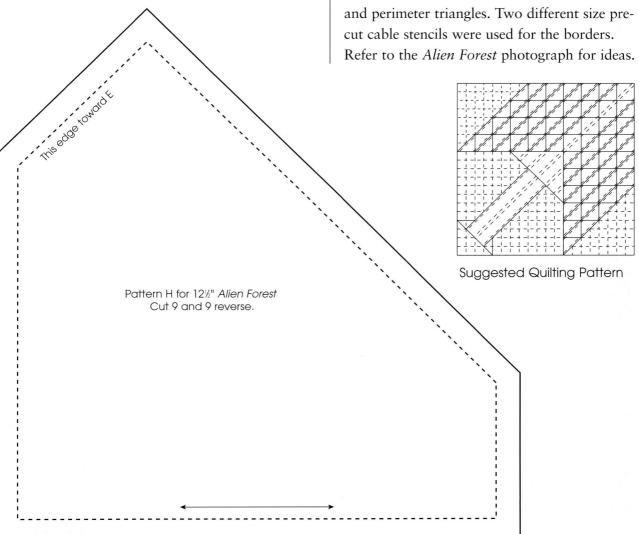

This edge toward E

Pattern H for 12½" *Alien Forest*
Cut 9 and 9 reverse.

Suggested Quilting Pattern

Need to make a gift in a hurry? Once you've collected the fabrics, *The Jewel Tree* can be designed, sewn, quilted, and framed—all in one day! Although it calls for a couple of Y-seams and several minuscule amounts of fabrics, the striking results are worth the effort. The double-layer mat and the black frame are ready-made so all you have to do is add the quilt. Instructions for framing are given on page 122.

Fabric Quantities

Work with scraps of the following solid color fabrics or create your own variation of the color scheme:

Block

Lighter Solids of Turquoise, Red-Violet, Lavender, Tan, Mustard, Peach, and 2 tints of Pink: 1 scrap (approximately 9" x 12") of each color for lighter-colored leaves and small squares

Darker Solids of Red-Violet, Bright Red, Kelly Green, Mustard, and 2 shades each of Turquoise, Green, and Purple: 1 scrap (approximately 9" x 9") of each color for darker-colored leaves

Red-Violet: 1 scrap (approximately 3½" x 5") for tree trunk

Background and Borders

Black: ⅜ yard

Binding: ¼ yard black. (No binding is necessary if you are planning to frame your quilt.)

Backing: ½ yard

Batting: 16" x 20"

Template plastic

Cutting

Refer to the Block Sewing Guide, page 96, and cut the following pattern pieces. Make a plastic template from The Jewel Tree Pattern F on page 96. If necessary, refer to Making and Using Templates on page 115.

Lighter and Darker Solids

- Cut 4 lighter-colored squares 1¼" x 1¼" (A).
- Cut 25 lighter-colored squares 1⅝" x 1⅝", then cut diagonally in half to make 50 lighter-colored triangles (B). (You will not use 1 triangle.)
- Cut 28 darker-colored squares 1⅝" x 1⅝", then cut diagonally in half to make 56 darker-colored leaf triangles (C).

Red-Violet

- Cut 1 square 3⅛" x 3⅛", then cut diagonally in half to make the tree trunk triangle (D). (You will not use 1 triangle.)
- Cut 1 rectangle 1 9/16" x 2⅝" for the tree trunk (E).

Note: To cut 1 9/16", align the edge of the fabric halfway between the 1½" and 1⅝" lines of the rotary cutting ruler.

Black

- Cut 2 pieces using template (F and F reversed) for background.
- Cut 2 squares 4⅛" x 4⅛", then cut diagonally in half for 4 corner triangles (G).
- Cut 2 crosswise strips 3" wide for border.

Note: You may want to cut the strips 3½"–4"wide if you are not framing the quilt. Doing this will provide room for a nice feather or cable quilting pattern in the border.

Designing the Block

Refer to *The Jewel Tree* Block Sewing Guide and place all the pieces on your design wall or board. Stand at least 10' away and decide if the

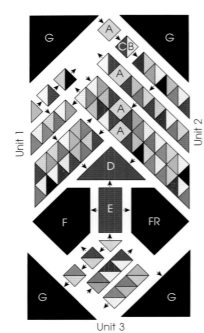

Unit 1

Unit 2

Unit 3

The Jewel Tree Block Sewing Guide

colors are living happily together. Does the block make a dramatic impact? If not, make substitutions.

Block Construction

1. Sew 40 B and 40 C triangles into squares to make the leaves in Units 1 and 2. Press toward the darker fabric and clip off the ears. Join the A and B/C squares into rows. Sew a single C triangle to the end of each row. Press in the direction of the arrows. Sew the rows of squares together. Press.

2. To make Unit 3, sew the tree root triangles together using the same method as the leaf triangles. Sew a single B triangle to the end of the top row. Press. Sew the rows together. Press. Attach the root triangle unit to the tree trunk (E). Set in the 2 adjoining background pieces F. Press. (See Sewing Inset Seams, page 119.) Add triangle D and the 2 G triangles. Press.

3. Sew Unit 1 to Unit 3. Press. Attach Unit 2. Press. Attach the 2 upper corner G triangles. Press.

Borders

1. Turn to Sewing Essentials, pages 117–118, for information on measuring and attaching borders.

2. Measure the width and length of the quilt top and trim the border strips to the appropriate lengths.

3. Attach side borders to the quilt and press toward the borders. Attach the top and bottom borders in the same manner.

Finishing

Turn to Sewing Essentials, pages 119–121, for finishing instructions. If you are planning to frame your quilt, binding is unnecessary.

Suggested Quilting

If you are not going to frame the quilt, you might want to do a nice cable or feather quilting pattern in the border.

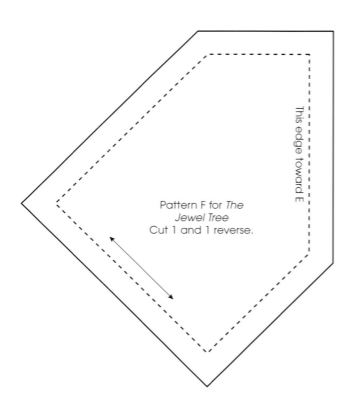

Pattern F for *The Jewel Tree*
Cut 1 and 1 reverse.

This edge toward E

Suggested Quilting Pattern

ONE-PATCH SQUARES

A square is the most common shape in quilting, but when it is combined with hundreds more of equal size, the effect can be spectacular! A square is used to make favorite traditional quilt patterns like Sunshine and Shadows and Trip Around the World. It can also be turned on-point to create the more contemporary Impressionist Landscapes I've been making for so many years. Squares can spell words or create pictorial shapes like the *Geometric Star* and the *Hearts and Flowers* quilts featured in this chapter.

Making a one-patch quilt can be a thoroughly artistic experience if you think of your design wall as a blank canvas waiting to be filled with a beautiful mosaic of colorful tiles. As each row of squares is put in place, the color relationships change and the pattern becomes more defined.

GEOMETRIC STAR

Geometric Star 69¼" x 69¼" (size before quilting), Gai Perry

A person might look at this quilt and wonder how in the world did she dream up the unusual color scheme? The answer is, I didn't. I used a *focus fabric*. I came across a floral print with an odd combination of colors that appealed to me. Then all I had to do was put together an assortment of prints and solids that were a reflection of the colors on the focus fabric.

This a large quilt so you will definitely need a design wall. If you don't have one, the alternative is to make an accurate paste-up, or design and sew it in four sections.

Color and Fabric Suggestions

The palette features a brilliant red solid color fabric to outline the center star and to define the rickrack border detail. Dark green print squares are positioned next to the red squares to enhance the contrast. The star is filled with light and bright prints in shades of turquoise, mustard, gold, salmon, and teal.

The background and the pieced border contain dark shades of brown, red, tan, teal, green, and turquoise. Many of these prints have touches of black in them. The inner border is defined with squares of another dark green print alternating with squares of a black-and-red star-patterned print.

Whatever palette you choose to recreate this star pattern, use the lightest, brightest, or darkest fabric to define the star and the border pattern.

Fabric Quantities

Common sense tells you that only a few inches of fabric are necessary for the square positions near the center of the star, so this list is just a starting point.

Blocks and Borders

Bright Red Solid: 1 yard of bright red solid for star outline and border detail

Dark Green Print: ¾ yard for star outline and border detail

Black-and-Red Print: ½ yard for border detail

Light- and Bright-Colored Solids and Prints: ¼ yard cuts (or large scraps) of 10 different fabrics for star interior

Medium- and Dark-Colored Prints: ⅓–⅝ yard cuts of 9 different fabrics to total 3 yards for background and border area

Binding: ½ yard of dark-colored print

Backing: 4⅛ yards

Batting: 74" x 74"

Cutting

This quilt contains 3,025 squares. Needless to say, a cut-as-you-design approach will seem less overwhelming.

Begin by cutting 2 crosswise strips 1¾" wide from all the fabrics you are considering for the interior of the star, except the squares close to the center. Then, cut the strips into 1¾" x 1¾" squares.

Designing the Quilt Top

Designing will be a trial-and-error effort so take a deep breath and jump in. Start by selecting 1 square of fabric for the center of the star and place it in the middle of your design wall. Then gradually work toward the star points. Cut more of each fabric as needed.

Note: It's okay to repeat some of the fabrics. Use the quilt photo and the *Geometric Star* Design Guide below as your reference for placement.

GEOMETRIC STAR

When you have finished designing the star, begin cutting squares for the background area. If you look at the quilt photo, you will see that the background fabrics are arranged in diagonal rows, and the colors are close in value to give the impression of a woven texture.

The illusion of an inner border is created with alternating squares of 2 dark prints. To design the pieced outer border, first position all the red and green squares (or whatever 2 colors you're working with), then fill in the remaining squares.

Quilt Top Construction

1. When every square is exactly where you want it, start sewing. Begin at the lower edge of the quilt and use the One-Pin, Two-Pin Sewing Method, pages 115–117, to sew each row of squares together. Alternate the pressing direction of the seams from row to row.

2. Join the rows and press all the seams in one direction.

Finishing

Turn to Sewing Essentials, pages 119–121, for finishing instructions.

Geometric Star Design Guide

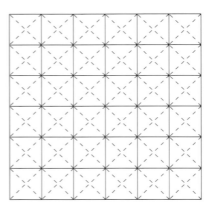

Suggested Quilting Pattern; overall diagonal grid

HEARTS
AND FLOWERS

Hearts and Flowers 46" x 54½" (size before quilting), Gai Perry. Machine Quilted by Connie Taxiera.

HEARTS AND FLOWERS

I dug into my collection of Impressionist Landscape florals to make this quilt, but if you're not wild about flowers, choose another theme like Valentine's Day prints, or maybe even a group of bird and butterfly prints.

Color and Fabric Suggestions

Hearts and Flowers has a multi-hued palette, but because pink was used for the border and to outline the hearts, it became the dominant color. Each of the hearts contains 3 prints from the same Color Family. The darkest print is next to the pink outline (or contour fabric) and the lightest print is in the middle of the heart. That was my idea in theory, but in some of the hearts, there is little distinction in value because I was intent on using only fabrics from my stash. Tints, tones, and shades of all six Color Families were used to make this quilt.

You will need a design wall for this pattern. If you don't have one, the alternative is an accurate paste-up.

Fabric Quantities

Hearts

There are 12 complete hearts and 3 partial hearts; each heart and partial heart contains scraps of 3 different prints.

Darker-Colored Floral Prints: 8" x 8" scrap of each of 15 fabrics

Medium-Colored Prints: 6" x 8" scrap of each of 15 fabrics

Lighter-Colored Floral Prints: 4" x 6" scrap of each of 15 fabrics

Background and Borders

Light-Colored Print: 1¼ yards for inner border. (You can get by with ¾ yard if you're willing to cut the borders crosswise and do some piecing.)

Tone-on-Tone, Textured Prints: 1½ yards total for the contour/outline squares and outer border. (If you're willing to cut the borders crosswise and do some piecing, you can get by with 1⅛ yards total; ⅜ for squares and ¾ for borders.)

Binding: ⅓ yard darker tone-on-tone, textured print

Backing: 2⅞ yards

Batting: 50" x 58"

Cutting

Hearts

The only sensible way to cut the hundreds of 2" x 2" squares required to make this scrap quilt is to cut squares as needed.

For each heart:

Darker-Colored Floral Prints
- Cut 16 squares 2" x 2" for each complete heart. Cut fewer squares for the partial hearts.

Medium-Colored Prints
- Cut 12 squares 2" x 2" for each complete heart. Cut fewer squares for the partial hearts.

Lighter-Colored Floral Prints
- Cut 5 squares 2" x 2".

Background and Borders

Light-Colored Prints
- Cut 5 crosswise strips 2" wide, then cut into 92 squares 2" x 2" for background.
- Cut 3 crosswise strips 2" wide or 2 lengthwise strips approximately 45" for the side inner borders.
- Cut 2 crosswise strips 2½" wide or 2 lengthwise strips 2½" x approximately 40" for the top and bottom inner borders.

Tone-on-Tone, Textured Print

◆ Cut 5 crosswise strips 2" wide, then cut 92 squares 2" x 2" for contour/outline of hearts.
◆ Cut 4 lengthwise strips 4½" x approximately 49" or 5 crosswise strips 4½" wide for outer border.

Designing the Quilt Top

Use the quilt photo on page 101 and the *Hearts and Flowers* Design & Construction Guide below as your road map for the placement of squares and color suggestions. For a quilt design like this, probably the most logical place to start is in the middle.

Select the scraps you want to use for the blue heart in the center. Arrange them on your design wall. If you like the results, put the contour squares around it and go on to the heart directly below it. Continue adding hearts and contour squares.

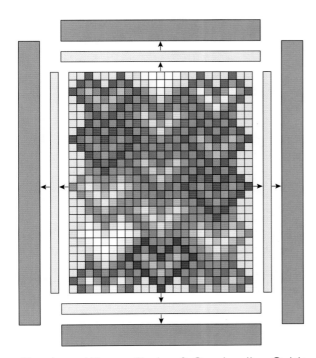

Hearts and Flowers Design & Construction Guide

Your eye is going to tell you whether or not the developing color scheme is working. Trust your instincts!

Quilt Top Construction

1. When every square is in place, start sewing. Begin at the lower edge of the quilt and use the One-Pin, Two-Pin Sewing Method, pages 115–117, to sew each row of squares together. Alternate the pressing direction of the seams from row to row.

2. Join the rows. Press all the seams in one direction.

Borders

1. Turn to Sewing Essentials, pages 117–118, for information on measuring and attaching borders.

2. Determine the width and length of the quilt top and trim all the border strips to the appropriate lengths.

3. Attach the sides of the inner border, and then the top and bottom. Press seams toward the border.

4. Attach the outer border in the same manner.

Finishing

Turn to Sewing Essentials, pages 119–121, for finishing instructions.

Suggested Quilting Pattern; overall meandering loop pattern

ORPHAN TWO-PATCHES

This is the most versatile Two-Patch block I've ever worked with...and apparently, it's unrecognized because I couldn't find it listed in any of my reference books. Well, in order to write about this wonderful little orphan, it needed a name, but what a weighty responsibility! How could I think of one that would compete with such lofty titles as Robbing Peter to Pay Paul, Crazy Ann, and Duck's Foot In the Mud?

I finally decided on Poor, Pitiful Pearl. It has a nice alliterative sound and it reminds me of my best friend. Whenever she goes on and on . . . complaining about her love-life, her job, the world in general . . . I tease her by telling her she sounds like Poor, Pitiful Pearl. This always gets a laugh and we change the topic of conversation to something more uplifting. So who knows? Maybe making a quilt with this block will have the same uplifting effect.

Anatomy of the Two-Patch Block

The block has only four pattern pieces; one large triangle, two small triangles, and one square. It's as easy as 1-2-3 to sew. On the flip side, a person could spend hours playing with different block sets. I think you will be surprised to learn that all three quilts in this chapter were made with the Poor, Pitiful Pearl block.

LEFTOVERS

Leftovers, 52½" x 62½" (size before quilting), Gai Perry

eftovers had a serendipitous beginning. I was making a large quilt with a controlled palette. Fabrics that I thought would work, didn't, and they ended up on the cutting room floor—literally. My sewing room was carpeted with rejects. I was feeling too lazy to put them away and besides, I loved looking at the happy jumble of colors and patterns. I decided it was easier to cut them all up and make a second quilt.

Color and Fabric Suggestions

The color scheme is a bold combination of barn red, gold, purple, black, and white. The strong light and dark value contrasts give the quilt a crisp, hard-edge look. All the fabrics are traditional plaids, checks, and small-scale prints. Each block uses two or three fabrics and in all but one block, the two smaller triangles are made with very light-colored prints.

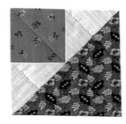

5" finished Poor, Pitiful Pearl (Two-Patch) block

Fabric Quantities

Work with the colors and fabric styles mentioned above and shown on the pattern quilt, or create your own variation of the pattern.

Blocks

Scraps, scraps, and more scraps. No more than ¼ yard each of any one fabric and include a range of light, medium, and dark colors in solids and traditional prints

Medium to Dark Scraps: approximately 2 yards total

Lightest Scraps: approximately 1 yard total

Borders and Binding

Inner Border: 1½ yards of pillow ticking stripe

Outer Border and Binding: 1⅔ yards of a bright or dark solid. (You can get away with ¾ yard if you are willing to cut crosswise and do some piecing.)

Backing: 3¼ yards

Batting: 56" x 66"

Cutting

Blocks

Refer to the 1–2–3 Block Sewing Guide, page 107, and cut the following pieces for each block. The following cutting method ensures a straight grain is stitched to a bias grain to prevent stretching. You will need 80 blocks.

Medium to Dark Scraps

◆ Cut 1 square 3" x 3" (#1). (You will need 80 total.)

◆ Cut 1 square 5⅞" x 5⅞", then cut diagonally in half to make 1 triangle (#3). Save the extra triangle for another block. (You will need 40 squares, 80 triangles total.)

Lightest Scraps

◆ Cut 1 square 4¾" x 4¾", then and cut diagonally in half in both directions to make 2 smaller triangles (#2). Save the 2 extra triangles for another block. (You will need 40 squares, 160 triangles total.)

Borders

Inner Border

◆ Cut 4 lengthwise strips 4" x 52".

Outer Border

◆ Cut 4 lengthwise strips 3" x 59" or cut 7 crosswise strips 3" wide.

Designing the Blocks

As I said before, this block is so quick to sew that it is easier to stitch them together before putting them on your design wall or board. When you sew a block you particularly like, make two or three more. The sharp focus of the blocks can be achieved by using very light-colored prints for the smaller triangles and by spreading the brightest and darkest large triangles equally across the surface of the quilt so that no particular area will stand out.

Block Construction

1. Sew the 2 smaller #2 triangles to a #1 square. Press in the direction of the arrows and clip off the ears.

2. Add a large #3 triangle. Press in the direction of the arrows and clip off the ears.

1-2-3 Block
Sewing Guide

Quilt Top Construction

1. When all the blocks are sewn, arrange them using the *Leftovers* Design & Construction Guide as a reference for the block set.

2. Start at the bottom and use the One-Pin, Two-Pin Sewing Method, pages 115–117, to sew each row of blocks together. Alternate the pressing direction of the seams from row to row.

3. Join the rows and press all the seams in one direction.

Borders

1. Turn to Sewing Essentials, pages 117–118, for information on measuring and attaching borders.

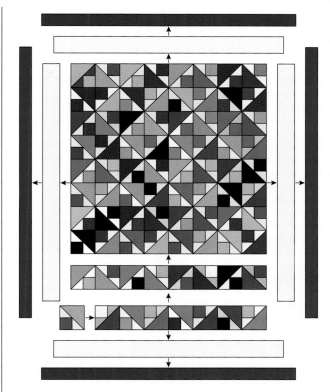

Leftovers Design & Construction Guide

2. Measure the width and length of the quilt top and trim all the border strips to the appropriate lengths. Attach the sides of the inner border, then the top and bottom. Press the seams toward the border.

3. Attach the outer border strips in the same manner.

Finishing

Turn to Sewing Essentials, pages 119–121, for finishing instructions.

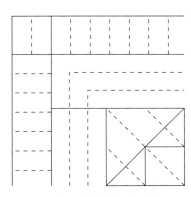

Suggested Quilting Pattern

WHO CUT UP
GREAT GRANNY'S DRAPES?

Who Cut Up Great Granny's Drapes?, 42½" x 50½" (size before quilting), Gai Perry. Machine quilted by Connie Texiera.

A flowery collection of vintage-style prints was used to make this softly-colored, pastel quilt. Wouldn't it look pretty hanging on a blanket rack or draped over the back of a wicker love seat?

Color and Fabric Suggestions

Ultra creamy tints of gray-blue, peach, cream, strawberry, cantaloupe, and avocado comprise the color scheme. This time Poor, Pitiful Pearl is set on a different angle in each of 4 quadrants to form a concentric diamond pattern.

4" finished Poor, Pitiful Pearl (Two-Patch) block

Fabric Quantities

Use the colors and fabric styles mentioned above and shown on the project quilt, or create your own variation.

Blocks

Pastel Prints: ¼ yard each or scraps that measure approximately 8" x 15" of 16 fabrics. (For this predominantly warm-colored quilt, the ratio is 12 warm-colored prints to 4 cool-colored prints. Assortment should include florals, polka dots, checks, and textures.)

Very Light Cream-Colored Prints: ⅛ yard each or scraps that measure approximately 9" x 13" of 8 fabrics

Borders

Inner Border: ¼ yard of light-colored print

Outer Border: 1¼ yards of large-scale floral print (You can get away with ¾ yard if you're willing to cut crosswise and do some piecing.)

Binding: ⅓ yard of small-scale floral print
Backing: 1⅞ yards
Batting: 46" x 54"

Cutting

Blocks

Refer to the Block Sewing Guide, page 110, and cut the following pattern pieces for each block. The following cutting method ensures a straight grain is stitched to a bias grain to prevent stretching. You will need 80 blocks.

Pastel Prints
◆ Cut 1 square 2½" x 2½" (#1). (You will need 80 total squares.)

Second Pastel Print
◆ Cut 1 square 4⅞" x 4⅞", then cut diagonally in half to make 1 triangle (#3). Save the extra triangle for another block. (You will need 40 squares for a total 80 triangles.)

Very Light Cream-Colored Prints
◆ Cut 1 square 4⅛" x 4⅛" from each of 2 different prints. Cut each square diagonally in half in both directions for the 2 smaller triangles (#2). Save the extras for another block. (You will need 40 squares for a total 160 triangles.)

Borders

Inner Border
◆ Cut 2 crosswise strips 1½" x 36" and 2 crosswise strips 1½" x approximately 42".

Outer Border
◆ Cut 4 lengthwise strips 4½" x 44" or cut 5 crosswise strips 4½" wide.

Designing the Blocks

Start by designing the 4 middle blocks and then work toward the outer edges of the quilt. I designed all the blocks before I started sewing because I wanted to make sure the few, cool-colored fabrics were evenly spaced across the surface of the quilt top. I also didn't want a cool-colored square in direct contact with a cool-colored large triangle. (Am I getting too fussy?) All right, just have fun designing a bunch of pretty blocks.

Block Construction

1. Sew 2 small #2 triangles to a #1 square. Press in the direction of the arrows and clip off the ears.

2. Add a large #3 triangle. Press in the direction of the arrows and clip off the ears.

1-2-3 Block
Sewing Guide

Quilt Top Construction

When all the blocks are sewn, arrange them using the *Who Cut Up Great Granny's Drapes?* Design & Construction Guide as a reference.

1. Start at the bottom and use the One-Pin, Two-Pin Sewing Method, pages 115–117, to sew each row of blocks together. Alternate the pressing direction of the seams from row to row.

2. Join the rows and press all the seams in one direction.

Borders

1. Turn to Sewing Essentials, pages 117–118, for information on measuring and attaching borders.

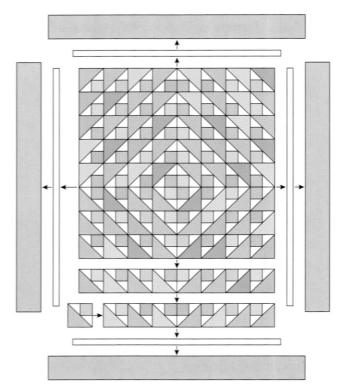

Who Cut Up Great Granny's Drapes? Design & Construction Guide

2. Measure the width and length of the quilt top and trim all the border strips to the appropriate lengths. Attach the sides of the inner border, then the top and bottom. Press the seams toward the border.

3. Attach the outer border strips in the same manner. Press seams toward the borders.

Finishing

Turn to Sewing Essentials, pages 119–121, for finishing instructions.

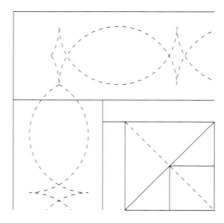

Suggested Quilting Pattern

NIGHT WINGS

Night Wings, Frame Size: 25" x 25", Quilt Size: 29½" x 29½" (size before quilting), Gai Perry

Here's the Poor, Pitiful Pearl Two-Patch block again, but what a difference the choice of fabrics and block set makes. To me, the quilt looks like a flock of geese racing through the night in a desperate attempt to stay ahead of a raging storm. To my oldest son, it looks like a bunch of light and dark triangles.

Color and Fabric Suggestions

The palette contrasts black, red-violet, purple, and rust with pale lavender, and a very light, violet-tinged texture. With the exception of the rust and the violet-tinged texture, all the fabrics are solid colors.

3" finished Poor, Pitiful Pearl (Two-Patch) block

Fabric Quantities

Work with the colors and fabric types mentioned above or develop you own variation of the pattern.

Blocks

Black: ¾ yard (A)

Darks or Dark-Brights: ⅛ yard each of
  3 fabrics (B, C, D)

Very Lights: ⅛ yard each of 2 fabrics (E, F)

Border: ½ yard

Binding (optional): ¼ yard

Backing: 1 yard

Batting: 33" x 33"

Cutting

Refer to the Block Sewing Guide, page 113, and cut the following pattern pieces. The following cutting method ensures a straight grain is stitched to a bias grain to prevent stretching. You will need 64 blocks.

Blocks

Black

Fabric A

◆ Cut 50 squares 2" x 2" (#1).

◆ Cut 32 squares 3⅞" x 3⅞", then cut diagonally in half to make 64 triangles (#3).

Darks or Dark-Brights

Fabric B

◆ Cut 14 squares 2" x 2" (#1).

Fabric C

◆ Cut 5 squares 3⅜" x 3⅜", then cut diagonally in half in both directions to make 20 triangles (#2).

Fabric D

◆ Cut 10 squares 3⅜" x 3⅜", then cut diagonally in half in both directions to make 40 triangles (#2).

Very Lights

Fabric E

◆ Cut 10 squares 3⅜" x 3⅜", then cut diagonally in half in both directions to make 40 triangles (#2).

Fabric F

◆ Cut 7 squares 3⅜" x 3⅜", then cut diagonally in half in both directions to make 28 triangles (#2).

Border

◆ Cut 4 crosswise strips 3" wide. (They will be trimmed later to accommodate the frame size.)

Designing the Blocks

Cut the pieces for all 64 blocks. Put them on your design wall or board before you start sewing. This will enable you to develop or change an emerging pattern. Use the *Night Wings* Design & Construction Guide as a reference for placement. When all the pieces are in place, sew the blocks.

Block Construction

1. Sew 2 small #2 triangles to a #1 square. Press in the direction of the arrows and clip off the ears.

2. Add a large #3 triangle. Press in the direction of the arrows and clip off the ears.

1-2-3 Block
Sewing Guide

Quilt Top Construction

1. Start at the bottom and use the One-Pin, Two-Pin Sewing Method, pages 115–117, to sew each row of blocks together. Alternate the pressing direction of the seams from row to row.

2. Join the rows. Press all the seams in one direction.

Borders

The border strips will be trimmed to accommodate the size of the precut framing strips. If you aren't planning to frame your quilt, cut wider border strips to allow for an attractive quilting pattern. Turn to Sewing Essentials, pages 118–119, for information on mitered borders.

Measure the width and length of the quilt top and trim each border strip an additional 10".

Finishing

Turn to Sewing Essentials, pages 119–121, for finishing instructions.

Framing Information

After quilting *Night Wings*, do not bind it. Heavy quilting will shrink the size of the quilt so it will fit perfectly within the mat opening. Turn to page 122 for easy framing instructions.

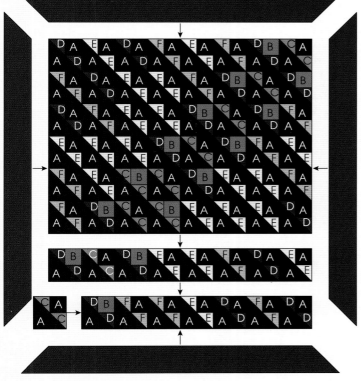

Night Wings Design & Construction Guide

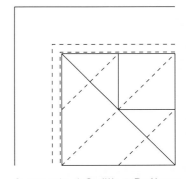

Suggested Quilting Pattern

SEWING
ESSENTIALS

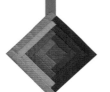

In this section, you will find explanations of sewing techniques that relate specifically to the quilts in this book. All the described procedures assume that you have an understanding of the basic sewing skills required to make a quilt. If you are a new quilter, there are excellent how-to books available (Reference Books, page 127).

PRESSING

I'm a big fan of pressing. There's something very satisfying about seeing an unpressed block turn into a crisp, unwrinkled piece of stitchery with flat, unobtrusive seam allowances. Also, it's my opinion that frequent and careful pressing will result in quilt tops that are flat and in-square.

Press As You Sew! Press triangles after stitching them into squares. Press each row of squares or blocks before and after joining them to the next row. Here's a pressing tip: Spread a large terry cloth bath towel across the top of your ironing board cover. Just like magic, it will help to prevent seam allowance ridges from showing through to the front of the quilt.

I know many of you were taught that steam is inappropriate, but I like lots of steam when I'm pressing. Whatever your preference, try not to stretch the fabric by constantly wiggling the iron back and forth. Put it straight down on the item you are pressing, hold it for a second or two, then gently move on.

CUTTING AND SEWING HALF-SQUARE AND QUARTER-SQUARE TRIANGLES

Almost all the patterns in this book require lots of triangles, so learn to measure and cut them accurately. When a quilt pattern calls for contrasting pairs of lighter- and darker-colored triangles, cut all the light-colored fabrics into quarter-square triangles; the dark-colored fabrics, into half-square triangles. Cutting this way ensures that a straight grain will be sewn to a bias edge and will keep the sewn triangle unit from stretching.

To make quarter-square triangles: Cut a square that is 1¼" larger than the finished measurement of the longest side of the triangle. Cut the squares diagonally in half in both directions to form 4 triangles.

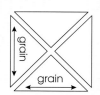

To make half-square triangles: Cut a square that is ⅞" larger than the finished measurement of one of the shorter sides of the triangle. Cut the square diagonally in half to form 2 triangles.

When sewing the pairs of triangles together, press toward the darker fabric, unless otherwise noted. Cut off the little ears for more accurate piecing.

MAKING AND USING TEMPLATES

To make an accurate template, you will need: clear or opaque template plastic; fine-point, permanent black ink pen; clear plastic ruler; and paper cutting scissors.

Place the template plastic over the desired pattern and put the edge of the ruler on top of the plastic, against the line you want to trace. Trace the line with a black pen. Repeat until all the lines are transferred to the plastic. Also trace the dotted seam lines so when you put the template on fabric you can see what will be lost in the seam allowance. Cut out the template and if you accidentally mess up, it's okay—but make another one. An imperfect template will give you sewing troubles you don't need.

When you are tracing a template on fabric, use a black, permanent-ink pen on light fabric and a white chalk wheel on dark fabrics. The alternate method is to work with a rotary cutter and mat. Use whichever method feels more comfortable.

ONE-PIN, TWO-PIN SEWING METHOD

When I developed the Impressionist Landscape series, I came up with a method for sewing rows of squares together that would automatically keep them in the right order. It's a fast, accurate (and no-brainer) way to sew straight or diagonal rows of squares together. It also works with straight or diagonal rows of blocks. The illustrated directions may look confusing, but if you follow them one step at a time, you will become an enthusiastic convert to the One-Pin, Two-Pin Sewing Method.

Sewing Straight Rows of Squares (or Blocks)

1. Begin by putting one pin in the left side of the first square (or block) on the left. This will be called the One-Pin Unit. Now put two pins in the right side of the far-thest right square (or block) in the row. This will be called the Two-Pin Unit.

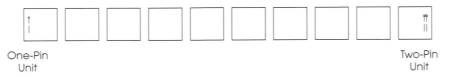

One-Pin
Unit

Two-Pin
Unit

2. Sew the square (or block) designated as the One-Pin Unit to the square (or block) sitting directly next to it. With the presser foot still down, sew a few more stitches and leave the unit in the machine.

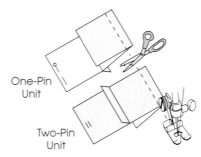

One-Pin
Unit

3. From the other end of the same row, pick up the square (or block) designated as Two-Pin Unit and sew it to the square (or block) directly next to it. With the presser foot still down, sew a few more stitches and leave the unit in the machine. With your scissors, detach the One-Pin Unit.

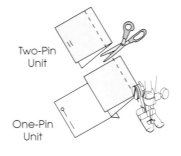

One-Pin
Unit

Two-Pin
Unit

4. Move back to the left side of the row and pick up the next square (or block) in sequence and sew it to the One-Pin Unit. With the presser foot still down, sew a few more stitches and then leave this unit in the machine. With your scissors, detach the Two-Pin Unit.

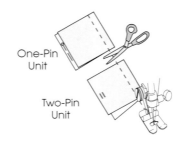

Two-Pin
Unit

One-Pin
Unit

5. Move back to the right side of the row and pick up the next square (or block) in sequence and sew it to the Two-Pin Unit. With the presser foot still down, sew a few more stitches and this leave this unit in the machine. With your scissors, detach the One-Pin Unit.

One-Pin
Unit

Two-Pin
Unit

6. Continue sewing in this manner until all the squares (or blocks) in the row are joined to the One-Pin or Two-Pin Units. Sew the 2 units together and pin the resulting strip on the your design wall, or board, in the correct position.

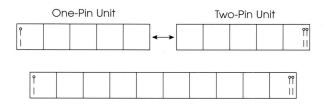

One-Pin Unit   Two-Pin Unit

Sewing Diagonal Rows of Squares (or Blocks)

Follow the steps described above. The only difference is that you will put the pins in the triangles at the beginning and end of each row.

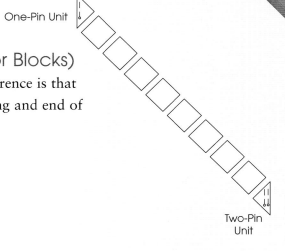

One-Pin Unit

Two-Pin Unit

SEWING STRAIGHT BORDERS

1. Carefully press the quilt top and lay it on a flat surface. With a ruler or measuring tape, determine the distance between points A and B. Note: It's best to measure from the center top to the center bottom because this is where the quilt will be the most narrow. Generally, there tends to be a little stretching along the outer edges.

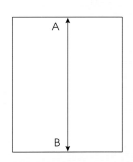

2. Cut 4 strips to the desired width of the border. Cut 2 of the 4 strips to the exact measurement of the length between A and B. Put a pin in the right and left center of the quilt top and a pin in the center of each of the 2 border strips.

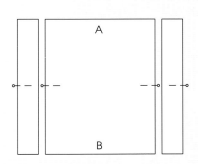

3. Match the pins and attach the border strips to the center points of the quilt top with the right sides facing the quilt. Now pin the end of the border strips to each corner of the quilt top. Fill in between the center and the corners with more pins. Ease if necessary. Sew the 2 border strips to the quilt top and press the seam allowances away from the quilt.

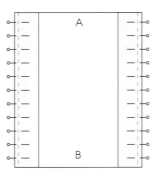

4. Measure the distance between points C and D and cut the 2 remaining border strips to that exact length. Put a pin in the top and bottom center of the quilt top and another pin in the center point of the 2 border strips, then repeat Step 3.

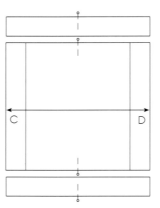

SEWING MITERED BORDERS

Border lengths should be cut the width and length of the quilt top, plus twice the combined widths of all the borders and an extra 3".

1. Sew border strips to the quilt top leaving a ¼" seam allowance at each corner unsewn. Backstitch to secure. Press seams toward the quilt.

Read five how-to books and you'll find five different ways to miter a border's corner. Here's the way I do it. It's less complicated because no measuring is involved.

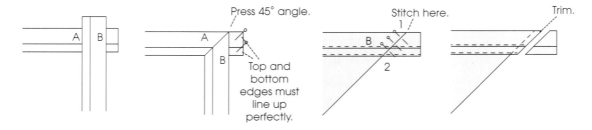

2. Place the corner section of the quilt that is going to be mitered on your ironing board. Position border strip B over border strip A.

3. Arrange the excess lengths of the border strips exactly as they are shown on the illustration and spear-pin to hold in place. Press the 45° angle that is created by folded strips.

4. Remove the pins and fold border strip B over border strip A. Place pins along the pressed line to keep the border strips from shifting and stitch between point 1 and 2. Backstitch to secure.

5. Trim the excess A and B border strips leaving a ¼" seam allowance. Press the seam open.

SEWING INSET SEAMS FOR *THE JEWEL TREE*

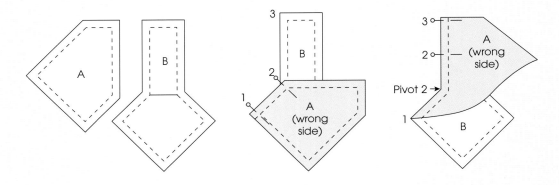

1. Place fabric A over fabric B (right sides together). Place pins at points 1 and 2 to secure. Using ¼" seams, sew from point 1 to point 2. Leave the sewing machine needle in the fabric.

2. Raise the presser foot and shift the fabrics. Pin between point 2 and point 3. Pivot fabrics under the needle. Lower the presser foot and continue sewing to point 3. Press toward fabric A. Repeat steps for the other side.

QUILTING AND FINISHING

Once your quilt top is sewn and carefully pressed, it's time to give it the supple texture and coziness that comes with quilting. Your first concern is a good quality, 100% cotton backing fabric. Choose a colorful print that will complement the style and theme of your quilt top (and one that is busy enough to hide any quilting flaws). The backing fabric should be larger than the quilt top by at least 5" in the width and length. With larger quilts, this will require some piecing.

PREPARING THE QUILT SANDWICH

Basting your quilt top requires a large flat surface. Most quilters have two choices, the dining room table or the floor. Since the floor isn't user-friendly to older bodies like mine, I prefer to work on a table. To extend its size, I tape two fold-out dressmaker boards together. The 72" x 72" surface protects my dining table and it's large enough to accommodate most wallhanging-size quilts.

After washing the backing fabric (or not washing, depending on your preference), press and spread it over the dressmaker's board, right side facing down. Secure it with masking tape. Next, in this quilt sandwich, comes the batting and I will give you my preferences in the quilting section that follows. Spread the batting over the backing fabric and smooth out any wrinkles.

If you are planning to machine quilt, you will need to mark the quilting pattern on your quilt top before basting. I do most of my quilting by hand and I like to mark the patterns as I quilt.

After marking the quilting pattern (or not), spread the quilt top over the batting. If you are hand quilting, use straight pins placed about every 4"–6" apart to temporarily secure the layers. For machine quilting, use #1 nickel-plated safety pins and place them no more than 3" apart.

BASTING AND HAND QUILTING

I love to quilt by hand, but who has the luxury of the countless hours it takes to complete a large quilt? If you are one of those lucky few people who have the time, you've probably devised a quilting routine that pleases you. If not, this is the way I do it.

My battings of choice are Mountain Mist Quilt Light (synthetic) and Fairfield Soft Touch (100% cotton). Both of these battings are thin and make the finished quilt look smooth and flat. They are also easy to "needle." After the quilt sandwich is pinned, I baste it with a radial pattern rather than a grid pattern. I do this because I lap quilt without a hoop and I've found the radial style keeps the backing fabric from bunching. If you want to try quilting without a hoop, which incidentally is much faster, just remember to start your stitches in the middle of the quilt and work toward the four corners.

I use 100% cotton quilting thread, and if I don't want the quilting stitches to be obvious, I change thread color from area to area.

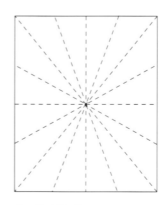

Radial Pattern

QUILTING BY MACHINE

I have started to do some machine quilting and I've learned that it is an art form all by itself! If you are just beginning to quilt by machine, the best advice I can give is to get Harriet Hargrave's book, *Heirloom Machine Quilting*. It's excellent! Of course, you can always send your quilt top to a professional to be quilted. It will save you precious hours of time and you will be doing your part to help boost the sagging economy.

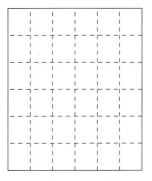

Grid Pattern

BINDING THE QUILT

My favorite bindings are made with plaids, stripes, or colorful prints that haven't been used anywhere else in the quilt. Sometimes I like to use more than one fabric for binding, so I prefer to make individual binding strips rather than a continuous binding. I also think individual binding strips look more professional—with perfect 90° corners.

Before attaching the binding, carefully press your quilt using a polyester setting. Never, never use a hot iron. The batting could melt! This procedure is like blocking a sweater; it eliminates any rippling and, somehow, it makes the quilting stitches look better.

Measure your quilt to see if it is still in square. Sometimes during the quilting process, the corners become slightly stretched. If this happens, trim them just enough to get the quilt back in square.

For straight binding strips: Cut 2"-wide fabric strips in lengths that are slightly longer than the width and length of the quilt. Sew the strips together for needed length, if necessary. Fold the strips in half and press. Using ¼" seams, machine stitch the raw edges of 2 of the strips to the right and left sides of the quilt. Trim the excess even with the quilt. Fold over and hand stitch to the back of the quilt. Repeat the process for the top and bottom of the quilt, folding in ¼" at each end before hand stitching to the back of the quilt.

FRAMING
INSTRUCTIONS

FRAMING THE QUILT

A frame should enhance the image it surrounds; not compete for attention. This is particularly true when it comes to framing a quilt. One can find almost any style of ready-made frame, but because there is so much action on the surface of a quilt (design, color, fabric pattern, and quilting stitches), I think simple frames are best.

The following information has been excerpted from my book, *Do-It-Yourself Framed Quilts*. The general information about ready-made framing materials is followed by individual framing requirements and easy, step-by-step instructions.

Ready-Made Framing Strips

All quilts in this book have been framed with metal framing strips. They are attractive, inexpensive, and very easy to assemble. Framing strips are available at most art supply and craft stores. The finished include silver, pewter, black, copper, and gold finishes.

Framing strips come two strips to a package, in lengths from 6"–40". You will have to buy one package for the length and another for the width, and everything needed to assemble the frame (except a screwdriver) is included.

Precut Mats

If you plan to frame a quilt that measures less than 16" x 20", a mat will make it look more important. Double layer mats are preferable because they will add an extra dimension of color, much like an inner and outer border. A double layer mat will also keep the glass from touching your quilt. This is important because a framed quilt must have some breathing space.

Package labeling should indicate that it is acid-free. An acid-free mat doesn't have chemicals which could eventually stain or yellow your quilt. When selecting a mat, make sure the opening is at least one inch smaller in width and length than the measurement of your quilt.

Foamcore Backing

This product is modestly priced and will provide a rigid surface on which to attach your quilt. Like the mat, it should also be labeled acid-free. A craft or framing store will cut it to your size specifications.

When To Use Glass

If you plan to mat your quilt picture, it would be advisable to use glass to keep the mat surface in pristine condition. If you plan to frame your quilt without a mat, glass isn't necessary.

Framing Supplies

Depending on how you plan to frame your quilt, some of the items in the following supply list will be needed to complete the project. Don't feel overwhelmed by the number of items. The framing process is really very easy. Trust me!

Note: Equipment is available at art, craft, and ready-made frame stores.

Framing strips (two packages: one for the length and one for the width)
Precut acid-free mat (double layer)
Acid-free tape or white linen tape
Sequin pins (½" long, straight pins)
Flat head screw driver
Acid-free, foamcore backing
Glass (if you are using a mat)
Picture wire

HOW TO FRAME A MATTED QUILT

Deco Medallion: Custom-cut double-layer mat. Opening measurement: 13½" x 13½"; outside measurement 20" x 20". (Sorry for the added expense, but square mats aren't available in precut sizes.) Two packages of 20" black framing strips. 20" x 20" picture glass. 20" x 20" foamcore backing. Acid-free tape.

The Jewel Tree: 11" x 14" precut double-layer mat. Packages of 11" and 14" black framing strips. 11" x 14" picture glass. 11" x 14" foamcore backing. Acid-free tape.

Note: See Ready-Made Framing Alternatives on page 126 for additional framing ideas.

1. Purchase a precut, double-layer mat and a width and length package of framing strips to match the size of the mat. You will also need the corresponding size glass and an acid-free foamcore backing.

2. Work on a clean, protected surface such as a cloth-covered dining table.

Place the quilt in the center of the foamcore backing and cover it with the mat. Now go back and forth, lifting the mat and adjusting the quilt until the part of the quilt you want

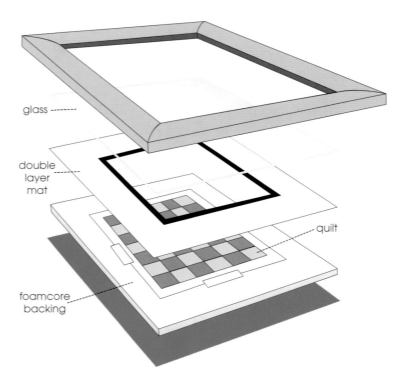

glass --------
double layer mat
quilt
foamcore backing

Exploded View of the Framing Sandwich (using a mat)

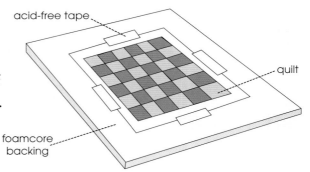

acid-free tape

quilt

foamcore backing

to show is centered under the mat. Carefully lift the mat one more time and put a piece of acid-free tape at four points around the edge of the quilt to secure its position. Replace the mat.

3. Clean the glass and make sure it is dry before putting it on top of the matted quilt.

4. Assemble the bottom and 2 sides of the framing strips according to package directions, but leave the fourth side open. Slide the mounted quilt, the mat, and the glass into the frame and then attach the fourth side.

5. Metal framing strips come packaged with special clips to hold the framing sandwich in place. Simply snap the clips into position. Attach the special screw eyes that are also included in the package.

6. Cut a piece of picture wire approximately 5" longer than the distance from eye to eye. Thread the wire into 1 of the screw eyes and wind the shorter end around itself 5 or 6 times. Stretch the wire across the frame and thread it into the other screw eye and wind to secure. Make sure the wire isn't so long that it will extend beyond the top of the frame when hanging on the wall.

HOW TO FRAME A QUILT WITHOUT A MAT AND GLASS

Making Waves: Two packages of 33" silver metal framing strips. 33" x 33" foamcore backing. Sequin pins. Picture wire.

Analogous Weave: Two packages of 35" x 35" silver metal framing strips. 35" x 35" foamcore backing. Sequin pins. Picture wire.

Night Wings: Two packages of 25" x 25" black metal framing strips. 25" x 25" foamcore backing. Sequin pins. Picture wire.

1. Measure the width and length of your quilt. (They may, or may not conform to the sizes I have given because of cutting and sewing variables.) Purchase packages of width and length framing strips that come the closest to the measurements of your quilt top, but not larger. For example, if your quilt measures 25½" x 25½", get 25" framing strips. Also, have a piece of acid-free foamcore backing cut to the exact size of the width and length of the strips.

2. Working on a clean, protected surface, attach the quilt to the foamcore backing. Because framing strips are always perfectly in square, and quilts rarely are, the process of attaching your quilt to a foamcore backing is an inexact science. This is how I do it.

Measure and mark the center point on each of the 4 perimeters of the foamcore backing. Now, put your quilt on top of the foamcore and, by "eye-balling" or measuring, line up the marks to correspond with the midpoints on your quilt. Note: At this point, your quilt will probably be a tad larger than the foamcore backing.

Temporarily secure your quilt to the center points on the foamcore with 4 regular size pins. Check to see if your quilt looks straight and if there is an equal amount of the edging strip border (if used) showing around the perimeters. If not, do some adjusting.

Working from the 4 center points to the corners, place sequin pins around the edge of the quilt. Push the pins in at an angle so they go through the quilt and into, but not all the way through, the foamcore. (Doing this is a little tricky.) Note: The pins will be covered by the lip of the frame. Once this is accomplished, trim any part of the quilt that extends over the edges of the foamcore.

3. Follow the same procedure as Steps 4–6 of the previous set of instructions, but omit the mat and glass.

READY-MADE FRAMING ALTERNATIVES

If the quilt you are planning to frame conforms to a standard size, there is an abundance of gallery style ready-made frames available to choose from. For information on standard sizes and framing techniques, shop craft, art supply, and framing stores, or read my book, *Do-It-Yourself Framed Quilts*.

REFERENCE BOOKS

Beyer, Jinny. *The Quilter's Album of Blocks and Borders*. McLean, VA: EPM Publications, Inc., 1980.

Fons, Marianne and Liz Porter. *Quilters Complete Guide*. Birmingham, AL: Oxmoor House, 1993.

Hargrave, Harriet. *Heirloom Machine Quilting*. Lafayette, CA: C&T Publishing, 1995.

LaBranche, Carol. *Patchwork Pictures*. Pittstown, NJ: The Main Street Press, Inc., 1985.

Leone, Diana. *The New Sampler Quilt*. Lafayette, CA: C&T Publishing, 1993.

McClun, Diana and Laura Nownes. *Quilts! Quilts!! Quilts!!!* Chicago, IL: The Quilt Digest Press, 1998.

McClun, Diana and Laura Nownes. *Quilts, Quilts, and More Quilts!* Lafayette, CA: C&T Publishing, 1993.

For quilting supplies:
Cotton Patch Mail Order
3405 Hall Lane, Dept.CTB
Lafayette, CA 94549
(800) 835-4418
(925) 283-7883

Email:quiltusa@yahoo.com
Website: www.quiltusa.com

Note: Fabrics used in the quilts shown may not be currently available since fabric manufacturers keep most fabrics in print for only a short time.

INDEX

ABOUT THE AUTHOR

Gai Perry began her romance with quilting in 1981 and she has been pursuing this passion ever since.

In 1985 Gai started teaching color and design at local quilt shops and seminars. Because of her fondness for antiques, her focus was on making traditional-style quilts. By 1990 she had a desire to start painting again, but instead of working with brushes, she developed an original style of quilting she named "The Art of the Impressionist Landscape." She has written two books on the subject.

In 1999 Gai wrote *Color From the Heart*; a fascinating collection of traditional color and design lessons and in 2001, *Do-It-Yourself Framed Quilts* was published. This is a project book containing design and framing instructions for Impressionist Landscapes and traditional quilts.

With the publication of this book, Gai says she is absolutely, positively going to get back into painting. We know all her students hope that she will take time out to teach classes and write more books!